The School for Scandal

Crofts Classics

GENERAL EDITORS

Samuel H. Beer, *Harvard University*

O. B. Hardison, Jr., *The Folger Shakespeare Library*

RICHARD
BRINSLEY SHERIDAN

The School
for Scandal

EDITED BY

John Loftis

STANFORD UNIVERSITY

AHM Publishing Corporation
Arlington Heights, Illinois 60004

Copyright © 1966
AHM PUBLISHING CORPORATION

All rights reserved

ISBN: 0-88295-092-4
(Formerly 390-23954-2)

Library of Congress Card Number: 66-12977

PRINTED IN THE UNITED STATES OF AMERICA

779

Eleventh Printing

INTRODUCTION

Sheridan's depiction in *The School for Scandal* of a benevolent man's triumph over a hypocrite illustrates the homely moral truth that love and charity more than prudence and the negative virtues determine a man's worth. This truth was popular in the eighteenth century, and so was the story that is its vehicle in the comedy: that of two brothers, the one dissolute but possessing the redeeming gift of charity and the other superficially decorous but in fact malignant, competing for a prize which is love and a fortune. *Tom Jones* is the most famous version of it, and in Fielding's novel as in Sheridan's play there is a paradoxical but indispensable sophistication of manner in the telling of the tale.

For all its celebration of the Christian virtue of benevolence, the play is an embodiment of the neoclassical reinterpretation of Aristotle's theory of comedy, just as it is an embodiment of neoclassical wit, as defined by Pope in *An Essay on Criticism*. A didactic play in its laughing and satirical rendering of the vice of scandalmongering, it focuses attention on a group of contemptible characters who illustrate the forms assumed by malicious hypocrisy. Its satirical target is as clearly defined as is that in a comedy of Molière, Ben Jonson, or Aristophanes, and that target represents the antithesis of the charity celebrated in the plot. The comedy is as neatly unified, in its satirical review of a vice and exemplary display of its corollary virtue, as a neoclassical critic could wish. The separate plot lines of Lady Teazle's marital dissatisfaction and Charles' and Joseph's competitive courtship of Maria converge in Sir Peter's discovery of his wife in Joseph's study; and if the chatter of Lady Sneerwell's circle fails to advance the action, it provides information about the relationship between the brothers Surface and the Teazle family and conveys a sense of the moral environment in which they live. Even the neoclassical unities of time and place are loosely observed, though in 1777, a decade after Dr. Johnson's famous assault on them in his Preface to Shakespeare, there could have been few critics to care whether Sheridan's imagined action took more than twenty-four hours or whether his imagined locales in fashionable London were close together.

Much more specifically neoclassical than neatness of construction is the conception of most of the characters as personifications of folly and vice, as representatives of a variety of aberrations (in a manner having at least a remote resemblance to Jonsonian humors) which are epitomized in their adjectival names. Lady Sneerwell and Lady Teazle are types of the general nature that Imlac recommended to the young Prince Rasselas, and they are lineal descendants of Congreve's Mrs. Frail and Lady Wishfort. Not subtle studies in motive or emotion, they are rather broadly and even boisterously drawn, comic renderings of the vices suggested by their names, embodiments of permanent if undesirable female qualities. Sheridan knew the neoclassical dramatic tradition, and however much he departed from the scheme of social and moral values observable in the Restoration plays, he followed that tradition in characterization—and in dialogue.

It is indeed in dialogue, in the linguistic virtuosity of his characters, that Sheridan most resembles the great comic dramatists of the late seventeenth century. He knew and admired Congreve, and more nearly than anyone else in the eighteenth century he approximated the stylistic accomplishment of *The Double-Dealer, Love for Love,* and *The Way of the*

World, in which the metaphorical texture of statement is of more consequence than primary meaning. Sheridan's characters, like Congreve's, strain for epigram, and often they achieve it, in expressions so neatly turned that a remark which is appropriate dramatically seems to articulate a thought that has occurred to many people at many times. "I'm called away by particular business," says Sir Peter, "but I leave my character behind me," and the thought, if not the phrase, has been in other minds in comparable situations. The characters achieve their effects, not by extravagance of conceit or unusual boldness of metaphor, but by common images used in unexpected ways; and they thereby make judgments of unexpected acerbity. The dialogue resembles familiar conversation in its separate components, but it is syntactically much more carefully contrived than even the best conversation, and it scores its ironical points with more regularity than the greatest wit ever did in unpremeditated repartee. The neoclassical fondness for parallelism and antithesis is apparent, and as we read the elaborate but closely controlled prose we find it easy to understand why Dr. Johnson himself proposed Sheridan for membership in The Club.

We could object to the dialogue, as critics have objected to Congreve's, on the grounds that it is too consistently witty to function effectively as a means of characterization. Such differentiation as exists in conversational ability is to the advantage of the malicious and hypocritical, for they enjoy the more uninhibited use of their faculties. Unlike Congreve, who gives a conversational advantage to his true wits, Sheridan shows the superior merits of his sympathetic characters by their deeds, though they too display a capacity for the clever phrase. And so, finally, his play does not (and here it differs from *The Way of the World*) convey a reverence for good conversation as the highest of the arts of civilization.

The comparison of *The School for Scandal* to *The Way of the World* is perennial and inevitable, a consequence of their shared qualities of dialogue and common preoccupation with slander and reputation. They are, in their separate centuries, the best of the comedies of manners—comedies, that is, having the depiction of the manners of fashionable society as their primary resource. Yet it is an oversimplification amounting to a distortion of fact to emphasize their similarities without differentiating them as representative of two distinct phases of dramatic history. If Sheridan's comedy, like Congreve's, is neoclassical in tidiness of construction, characterization, laughing and satirical approach to didactic objective, and aphoristic summaries of experience, it is different in social assumptions and moral evaluations, so different in fact that we may more conveniently regard it as representing a separate dramatic tradition. The difference between the two plays represents something like a transvaluation of a common set of dramatic conventions. As conversational ability and social finesse are the qualities by which conduct is measured in *The Way of the World*, benevolence—something very like the New Testament conception of charity—is the decisive, normative quality in *The School for Scandal*. We are called on to forgive Mirabell his relations with Mrs. Marwood and Mrs. Fainall and other loves and deceits too numerous to mention, because he has the redeeming gift of wit, understood as a clarity of mind finding expression in cleverness of phrase and adroitness in social relationships. We are asked to forgive Charles Surface his improvidence and profligacy, because he has the redeeming gift of charity. Mirabell deserves and wins the principal prize, Millamant and her fortune, not because he shows gratitude for past favors or sympathy with the unfortunate, but because he is the cleverest and most articulate male in the play. Charles Surface, on the other hand, exhibiting no conspicuous intelligence in the conduct of his affairs, deserves and wins Maria and his uncle's fortune because in a test situation he and not his brother responds with gratitude for past favors and with generosity to a man he believes to be distressed. Mirabell, in brief, is a wit and Charles is a man of feeling; between them and the ethical systems they epitomize stretches the long and complex history of eighteenth-century sentimentalism.

The word "sentimental" is used prominently in *The School for Scandal* as a term of derogation to describe the hypocritical fondness of Joseph for moralistic platitudes. Of sentimentalism in this pejorative sense, implying a wilful exploitation of emotion, Sheridan is singularly free, and in fact the play is remarkable for the contrary qualities of sustained gaiety and satirical astringency. We need not belabor the meaning of a frequently misused word and argue, in opposition to Sheridan's manifest intention, that the play is indeed "sentimental." Yet the ethical assumptions controlling the implied evaluations of his characters are largely those responsible for the sentimental movement in eighteenth-century literature. Sheridan is at one with the sentimentalists in focusing attention on episodes that illustrate the presence or absence of benevolence in his characters. Like Sterne and Goldsmith he has the redeeming gifts of style, wit, and intelligence, but also like them—in *A Sentimental Journey* and *The Vicar of Wakefield*—he explores the principal theme of the writers we consider to be sentimentalists: the emotional responsiveness of some if not all men to the distresses of others. This perhaps is merely to say that Sheridan, however determined not to be overemphatic or clumsy in depicting situations of emotional intensity, was a man of his times, responding to human relationships like other writers of the later eighteenth century in a very different manner from that in which Congreve responded to them at the end of the seventeenth century.

Sheridan is tolerant of deviations from prudent behavior as the seventeenth-century dramatists were not. In the marriage of Sir Peter and Lady Teazle, we encounter a relationship—an elderly but rich man married to a beautiful young woman who had accepted him to escape an obscure and impoverished life—that is reminiscent of earlier comedy. It has indeed some similarity to the relationship between Mr. Fondlewife and Laetitia in Congreve's *The Old Bachelor* or even to that between Mr. Pinchwife and Margery in Wycherley's *The Country Wife*. The change in Lady Teazle, from quiet country girl before marriage to imperious gossip afterwards, reminds us of the change in "the silent woman" of Jonson's *Epicene*; and the rapidity with which Lady Teazle acquires the skills of a coquette recalls the education of Agnès, Arnolphe's intended wife in Molière's *L'Ecole des femmes*. Unlike Sheridan, the seventeenth-century dramatists were uniformly severe in their satirical handling of an old man's folly in aspiring to marriage with a young girl. Sir Peter seems destined for cuckoldry as surely as were Fondlewife and Pinchwife. Yet the event is otherwise, and it is a measure of the distance between Sheridan and the earlier comedy.

Saved by accident from compromising herself (in the screen scene), Lady Teazle overhears Sir Peter explaining the generous provisions he has made for her financial security; and like many another character of the eighteenth-century sentimental tradition she is brought by this experience of magnanimity to an understanding of her folly and to a resolution to amend her conduct. Sheridan's difference from Congreve and Wycherley is partly a matter of increased restraint in portraying sexual relationships. But much more is involved, above all a greater tolerance and kindliness in handling aberrations from prudent and rational norms of conduct. Despite the matrimonial harmony established between Sir Peter and Lady Teazle at the end of the play, they remain a couple ill-matched in age and temperament. Sir Peter's initial indiscretion in marrying a very much younger woman is not and cannot be remedied; it is merely forgiven, and we are implicitly asked to believe that it no longer matters greatly. Sheridan indeed treats Sir Peter as a kind of later Sir Roger de Coverley, in whom folly and imperceptiveness become endearing qualities because they are consequences of emotional spontaneity.

Yet notwithstanding the indulgence shown to Sir Peter in his marriage—and to Charles Surface in his improvidence and dissipation—the tone of the play is not sentimental. That this is so is to be attributed to the scandal scenes that recur like a thematic refrain. Sheridan's indignation at calculated scandal-mongering, especially the published kind appearing in such journals as *The Town and Country Magazine* mentioned by Snake, gives timeliness and force to his social satire. The scandal scenes are thematically relevant in much the same way that the mad banter is in *King Lear*. The neatly turned epigrams of the gossips, in which malice is bearable because it is clever, establish the milieu in which the characters live out their lives. Just as the calculated double talk of the fool and the involuntary babble of the deranged king in *King Lear* pose questions concerning the rationality of destiny, so does the malice of the gossips in *The School for Scandal* pose questions concerning human benevolence. And so, by way of a contrast between the scandalmongers and the men of good will, there is established the distinctive tone of the play, that neat balance between sentiment and satire typical of the Age of Johnson at its very best.

In March 1777, two months before the first performance of *The School for Scandal,* Dr. Johnson proposed Sheridan for membership in The Club. "He who has written the two best comedies of his age," Johnson said, referring to *The Rivals* and *The Duenna,* "is surely a considerable man." Yet however considerable, he was not yet twenty-six years old; and in fact when his final important play, *The Critic,* was produced in 1779, he was still only twenty-eight. Prolific and precocious he was; we are reminded of Congreve by his age when his plays were first performed as by so much else in his career. The speed with which he won his fame, however, should not convey the false impression that he wrote hastily and facilely. On the contrary, the firm evidence of his work drafts of *The School for Scandal* reveals a slow and even laborious evolution of the play, of movement from collected scraps of the dialogue of gossips to two tentative plots (the one with a focus on Lady Sneerwell's circle and the other on the affairs of Sir Peter Teazle's family) and finally to a fusion of the two plots and an incorporation in the single comedy of the best phrases and situations from the early fragments. Sheridan's biographer, Thomas Moore (the poet and friend of Byron), printed extended passages from the drafts that enable us to follow the dramatist's progress toward the final form of the comedy. We see Sheridan collecting and relishing phrases, much as Swift did in compiling his *Complete Collection of Genteel and Ingenious Conversation,* though with the difference that Swift searched for banality and Sheridan for malice. All we know about the composition of *The School for Scandal* (and about its publication, as will be shown) suggests a kind of stylistic perfectionism—which proved to be fully justified by the success of the play.

The initial run of *The School for Scandal* was a triumph. Audiences as well as critics were delighted, and from the first performance on May 8, 1777, until the end of the theatrical season in early June, the comedy drew full houses. Sheridan had known and taken into account as he wrote it the special abilities of the actors and actresses, with the result that there was an unusual harmony between individual and role. Horace Walpole said that more parts were well acted in it than in any other play he could remember. Not only in the first season but for several years receipts from it were consistently higher than for other plays. In 1779 the Treasurer of the company noted that it had "damped the new pieces." And the success has endured. From that first season to the present, it has retained its life on the stage, a distinction the more impressive because it is shared by so few eighteenth-century plays.

Its success notwithstanding, Sheridan did not authorize its publication, presumably because he could never bring himself to regard the dialogue as having been brought to its final state of perfection. Yet a comedy so successful was inevitably printed, and often printed, without authorization. The texts of the early editions differ from one another, depending on their separate origins, and the result has been a complicated bibliographical problem for editors of Sheridan's works.

A generation ago the problem was simplified—and to some extent solved—when the late Professor George H. Nettleton identified a manuscript copy of the play, now in the Riggs Memorial Library of Georgetown University, as that which Sheridan presented to Mrs. Crewe, having corrected it in his own handwriting. Professor Nettleton published his transcription of the manuscript in 1939, in an anthology edited by himself and Arthur E. Case, *British Dramatists from Dryden to Sheridan* (Houghton Mifflin Company). With the generous permission of Georgetown University and Houghton Mifflin Company, the text of the Crewe manuscript as transcribed and (in rare instances) emended by Professor Nettleton is followed in the present edition. All departures from or additions to the Crewe manuscript are set off by brackets.

PRINCIPAL DATES IN
THE LIFE OF SHERIDAN

1751   Richard Brinsley Sheridan born in Dublin, October 30, the son of Thomas Sheridan, an actor and teacher of elocution, and his wife, a playwright and novelist. Grandson of the Rev. Thomas Sheridan, D.D., friend and biographer of Swift.

1762-1768   Attended Harrow School.

1770   Family settled at Bath, where Thomas Sheridan established an Academy of Oratory.

1772   Escorted Elizabeth Ann Linley, the beautiful daughter of a musician, to France so that she could escape the unwelcome attentions of Thomas Mathews. After returning to England Sheridan fought two duels with Mathews, in the second of which he was severely wounded.

1773   Married Miss Linley, April 13. Settled in London.

1775   *The Rivals* was produced with little success at Covent Garden, January 17. It was withdrawn, revised, and produced again, January 28, this time successfully. Reputation established when the comic opera, *The Duenna*, had an unprecedented run of seventy-five performances beginning November 21.

1776   In partnership with his father-in-law and a physician, gained control of the Theatre Royal, Drury Lane, on the retirement of David Garrick.

1777   Adaptation of Vanbrugh's *The Relapse* presented as *A Trip to Scarborough*, February 24. Elected a member of The Club, March 14, on

xv

the nomination of Dr. Johnson. *The School for Scandal* began a brilliant run of twenty performances, May 8.

1779   *The Critic*, a burlesque of theatrical abuses, first acted, October 30.

1780   Elected to Parliament. Remainder of career mainly devoted to public affairs.

1787   Established a great reputation for oratory with a speech in Parliament, February 7, against Warren Hastings.

1792   His wife died.

1794   New Drury Lane Theatre opened, April 21.

1795   Married Esther Ogle, daughter of the Dean of Winchester, April 27.

1799   *Pizarro*, an adaptation from the German of Kotzebue, first acted, May 24, 1799.

1806   Appointed Treasurer of the Navy in the "Ministry of all the Talents."

1809   Drury Lane Theatre burned, February 24, with disastrous financial consequences.

1813   Arrested for debt.

1816   Died, July 7. Buried in Poet's Corner, Westminster Abbey.

A PORTRAIT;

Addressed to Mrs. Crewe, with the Comedy
of The School for Scandal[1]

By R. B. SHERIDAN, Esq.

Tell me, ye prim adepts in Scandal's school,
Who rail by precept, and detract by rule,
Lives there no character, so tried, so known,
So decked with grace, and so unlike your own,
That even you assist her fame to raise,
Approve by envy, and by silence praise!
Attend!—a model shall attract your view—
Daughters of calumny, I summon you!
You shall decide if this a portrait prove,
Or fond creation of the Muse and Love.   10
Attend, ye virgin critics, shrewd and sage,
Ye matron censors of this childish age,
Whose peering eye and wrinkled front declare
A fixed antipathy to young and fair;
By cunning, cautious; or by nature, cold,
In maiden madness, virulently bold!
Attend, ye skilled to coin the precious tale,
Creating proof, where innuendos fail!
Whose practised memories, cruelly exact,
Omit no circumstance, except the fact!—   20
Attend, all ye who boast,—or old or young,—
The living libel of a slanderous tongue!
So shall my theme as far contrasted be,
As saints by fiends or hymns by calumny.
Come, gentle Amoret[2] (for 'neath that name
In worthier verse is sung thy beauty's fame),
Come—for but thee who seeks the Muse? and while
Celestial blushes check thy conscious smile,
With timid grace and hesitating eye,

[1] These dedicatory verses to Mrs. (later Lady) Crewe, a beautiful woman and a celebrated hostess, were sent to her with a
manuscript copy of the play   [2] Amoret Fox had praised Mrs.
Crewe as Amoret in a poem printed in 1775

30   The perfect model which I boast supply:—
Vain Muse! couldst thou the humblest sketch create
Of her, or slightest charm couldst imitate—
Could thy blest strain in kindred colors trace
The faintest wonder of her form and face—
Poets would study the immortal line,
And Reynolds own *his* art subdued by thine;
That art, which well might added lustre give
To nature's best and heaven's superlative:
On Granby's[3] cheek might bid new glories rise,

40   Or point a purer beam from Devon's[4] eyes!
Hard is the task to shape that beauty's praise,
Whose judgment scorns the homage flattery pays?
But praising Amoret we cannot err,
No tongue o'ervalues heaven, or flatters her!
Yet she by fate's perverseness—she alone
Would doubt our truth, nor deem such praise her own!
Adorning fashion, unadorned by dress,
Simple from taste, and not from carelessness;
Discreet in gesture, in deportment mild,

50   Not stiff with prudence, nor uncouthly wild:
No state has Amoret; no studied mien;
She frowns no *goddess*, and she moves no *queen*,
The softer charm that in her manner lies
Is framed to captivate, yet not surprise;
It justly suits th' expression of her face,—
'Tis less than dignity, and more than grace!
On her pure cheek the native hue is such,
That, formed by heaven to be admired so much,
The hand divine, with a less partial care,

60   Might well have fixed a fainter crimson there,
And bade the gentle inmate of her breast—
Inshrinèd Modesty—supply the rest.
But who the peril of her lips shall paint?
Strip them of smiles—still, still all words are faint!
But moving Love himself appears to teach
Their action, though denied to rule her speech;
And thou who seest her speak, and dost not hear,
Mourn not her distant accents 'scape thine ear;

[3] **Granby's** the Marchioness of Granby's   [4] **Devon's** the Duchess
of Devonshire's

Viewing those lips, thou still may'st make pretense
To judge of what she says, and swear 'tis sense: 70
Clothed with such grace, with such expression fraught,
They move in meaning, and they pause in thought!
But dost thou farther watch, with charmed surprise,
The mild irresolution of her eyes,
Curious to mark how frequent they repose,
In brief eclipse and momentary close—
Ah! seest thou not an ambushed Cupid there,
Too tim'rous of his charge, with jealous care
Veils and unveils those beams of heav'nly light,
Too full, too fatal else, for mortal sight?   80
Nor yet, such pleasing vengeance fond to meet,
In pard'ning dimples hope a safe retreat.
What though her peaceful breast should ne'er allow
Subduing frowns to arm her altered brow,
By Love, I swear, and by his gentle wiles,
More fatal still the mercy of her smiles!
Thus lovely, thus adorned, possessing all
Of bright or fair that can to woman fall,
The height of vanity might well be thought
Prerogative in her, and Nature's fault.   90
Yet gentle Amoret, in mind supreme
As well as charms, rejects the vainer theme;
And, half mistrustful of her beauty's store,
She barbs with wit those darts too keen before:—
Read in all knowledge that her sex should reach,
Though Greville,[5] or the Muse, should deign to teach
Fond to improve, nor tim'rous to discern
How far it is a woman's grace to learn;
In Millar's dialect[6] she would not prove
Apollo's priestess, but Apollo's love,   100
Graced by those signs which truth delights to own,
The timid blush, and mild submitted tone:
Whate'er she says, though sense appear throughout,
Displays the tender hue of female doubt;
Decked with that, charm how lovely wit appears,
How graceful *science,* when that robe she wears!

---

[5] **Greville** Mrs. Crewe's mother, Mrs. Fulke Greville   [6] **Millar's dialect** a contemptuous allusion to a Lady Millar, who conducted a literary salon near Bath

Such too her talents, and her bent of mind,
As speak a sprightly heart by thought refined:
A taste for mirth, by contemplation schooled,
100   A turn for ridicule, by candor ruled,
A scorn of folly, which she tries to hide;
An awe of talent, which she owns with pride!
    Peace, idle Muse! no more thy strain prolong,
But yield a theme, thy warmest praises wrong;
Just to her merit, though thou canst not raise
Thy feeble verse, behold th' acknowledged praise
Has spread conviction through the envious train,
And cast a fatal gloom o'er Scandal's reign!
And lo! each pallid hag, with blistered tongue,
110   Mutters assent to all thy zeal has sung—
Owns all the colors just—the outline true:
Thee my inspirer, and my *model*—CREWE!

PROLOGUE

Spoken by Mr. King[1]

Written by D. Garrick, Esq.

A School for Scandal! tell me, I beseech you,
Needs there a school this modish art to teach you?
No need of lessons now, the knowing think—
We might as well be taught to eat and drink.
Caused by a dearth of scandal, should the vapors
Distress our fair ones—let 'em read the papers;
Their pow'rful mixtures such disorders hit;
Crave what they will, there's *quantum sufficit.*[2]
   'Lord!' cries my Lady Wormwood (who loves tattle,
And puts much salt and pepper in her prattle),   10
Just ris'n at noon, all night at cards when threshing
Strong tea and scandal—'Bless me, how refreshing!
Give me the papers, Lisp—how bold and free! (*Sips.*)
Last night Lord L—— (sips) was caught with Lady D——
For aching heads what charming sal volatile! (*Sips.*)
If Mrs. B.——will still continue flirting,
We hope she'll DRAW, *or we'll* UNDRAW *the curtain.*
Fine satire, poz[3]—in public all abuse it,
But, by ourselves (*sips*), our praise we can't refuse it.
Now, Lisp, read *you*—there, at that dash and star.'[4]   20
   'Yes, ma'am.—*A certain Lord had best beware,*
Who lives not twenty miles from Grosv'nor Square;
For should he Lady W——find willing,
WORMWOOD *is bitter'*——'Oh! that's me! the villain!
Throw it behind the fire, and never more
Let that vile paper come within my door.'—
   Thus at our friends we laugh, who feel the dart;
   To reach our feelings, we ourselves must smart.
   Is our young bard so young, to think that he
   Can stop the full spring-tide of calumny?   30

---

[1] **Mr. King** Thomas King, who had the role of Sir Peter Teazle
[2] **quantum sufficit** as much as suffices   [3] **poz** positively   [4] **dash
and star** referring to the practice of partly obscuring names in
publishing reports of scandal

Knows he the world so little, and its trade?
Alas! the devil is sooner raised than laid.
So strong, so swift, the monster there's no gagging:
Cut Scandal's head off—still the tongue is wagging.
Proud of your smiles once lavishly bestow'd,
Again your young Don Quixote takes the road:
To show his gratitude, he draws his pen,
And seeks this hydra, Scandal, in his den.
For your applause all perils he would through—
40 He'll fight—that's *write*—a cavalliero true,
Till every drop of blood—that's *ink*—is spilt for you.

DRAMATIS PERSONAE

MEN

SIR PETER TEAZLE	*Mr. King*
SIR OLIVER SURFACE	*Mr. Yates*
JOSEPH SURFACE	*Mr. Palmer*
CHARLES SURFACE	*Mr. Smith*
CRABTREE	*Mr. Parsons*
SIR BENJAMIN BACKBITE	*Mr. Dodd*
ROWLEY	*Mr. Aickin*
TRIP	*Mr. LaMash*
MOSES	*Mr. Baddeley*
SNAKE	*Mr. Packer*
CARELESS	*Mr. Farren*

and other Companions to CHARLES [SURFACE],
Servants, etc.

WOMEN

LADY TEAZLE	*Mrs. Abington*
MARIA	*Miss P. Hopkins*
LADY SNEERWELL	*Miss Sherry*
MRS. CANDOUR	*Miss Pope*

[SCENE—LONDON]

THE SCHOOL FOR SCANDAL

Act I

Scene I

[Lady Sneerwell's *house*.]

Lady Sneerwell *at the dressing-table—*
Snake *drinking chocolate.*

Lady Sneer. The paragraphs, you say, Mr. Snake, were all inserted?

Snake. They were, madam, and as I copied them myself in a feigned hand, there can be no suspicion whence they came.

Lady Sneer. Did you circulate the reports of Lady *Brittle's* intrigue with Captain *Boastall?*

Snake. That is in as fine a train as your ladyship could wish,—in the common course of things, I think it must reach Mrs. *Clackit's* ears within four-and- 10 twenty hours; and then, you know, the business is as good as done.

Lady Sneer. Why, truly, Mrs. *Clackit* has a very pretty talent, and a great deal of industry.

Snake. True, madam, and has been tolerably successful in her day:—to my knowledge, she has been the cause of six matches being broken off, and three sons being disinherited, of four forced elopements, as many close confinements, nine separate maintenances, and two divorces;—nay, I have more than once 20 traced her causing a *Tête-à-Tête* in the *Town and*

Country Magazine,[1] when the parties perhaps had never seen each other's faces before in the course of their lives.

LADY SNEER. She certainly has talents, but her manner is gross.

SNAKE. 'Tis very true,—she generally designs well, has a free tongue, and a bold invention; but her coloring is too dark, and her outline often extravagant. She
30 wants that *delicacy* of *hint*, and *mellowness* of *sneer*, which distinguish your ladyship's scandal.

LADY SNEER. Ah! you are partial, Snake.

SNAKE. Not in the least; everybody allows that Lady *Sneerwell* can do more with a *word* or a *look* than many can with the most labored detail, even when they happen to have a little truth on their side to support it.

LADY SNEER. Yes, my dear Snake; and I am no hypocrite to deny the satisfaction I reap from the success
40 of my efforts. Wounded myself, in the early part of my life, by the envenomed tongue of slander, I confess I have since known no pleasure equal to the reducing others to the level of my own injured reputation.

SNAKE. Nothing can be more natural. But, Lady Sneerwell, there is one affair in which you have lately employed me, wherein, I confess, I am at a loss to guess your motives.

LADY SNEER. I conceive you mean with respect to
50 my neighbor, Sir Peter Teazle, and his family?

SNAKE. I do; here are two young men, to whom Sir Peter has acted as a kind of guardian since their father's death; the elder possessing the most amiable character, and universally well spoken of; the youngest, the most dissipated and extravagant young fellow in the kingdom, without friends or character,—the former an avowed admirer of your ladyship, and ap-

[1] the Town and Country Magazine specialized in reporting the intrigues of prominent persons

parently your favorite; the latter attached to Maria,
Sir Peter's ward, and confessedly beloved by her. Now,
on the face of these circumstances, it is utterly unac-   60
countable to me, why you, the widow of a city knight,
with a good jointure, should not close with the passion
of a man of such character and expectations as Mr.
Surface; and more so why you should be so uncom-
monly earnest to destroy the mutual attachment sub-
sisting between his brother *Charles* and *Maria.*

LADY SNEER. Then, at once to unravel this mystery,
I must inform you that love has no share whatever
in the intercourse between Mr. *Surface* and me.

SNAKE. No!   70

LADY SNEER. His real attachment is to *Maria,* or her
fortune; but, finding in his brother a favored rival, he
has been obliged to mask his pretensions, and profit
by my assistance.

SNAKE. Yet still I am more puzzled why you should
interest yourself in his success.

LADY SNEER. Heav'ns! how dull you are! Cannot you
surmise the weakness which I hitherto, through shame,
have concealed even from *you?* Must I confess that
Charles—that libertine, that extravagant, that bank-   80
rupt in fortune and reputation—that he it is for whom
I am thus anxious and malicious, and to gain whom
I would sacrifice everything?

SNAKE. Now, indeed, your conduct appears consis-
tent; but how came you and Mr. *Surface* so confiden-
tial?

LADY SNEER. For our mutual interest. I have found
him out a long time since—I know him to be artful,
selfish, and malicious—in short, a sentimental knave.

SNAKE. Yet, Sir Peter vows he has not his equal in   90
England—and, above all, he praises him as a man of
sentiment.

LADY SNEER. True; and with the assistance of his
sentiment and hypocrisy he has brought him [Sir
Peter] entirely into his interest with regard to *Maria.*

Enter Servant.

SERV. Mr. Surface.

LADY SNEER. Show him up.   *Exit Servant.*
He generally calls about this time. I don't wonder at
people's giving him to me for a lover.

Enter JOSEPH SURFACE.

100   JOS. SURF. My dear Lady Sneerwell, how do you
do to-day? Mr. Snake, your most obedient.

LADY SNEER. Snake has just been arraigning me on
our mutual attachment, but I have informed him of
our real views; you know how useful he has been to
us; and, believe me, the confidence is not ill placed.

JOS. SURF. Madam, it is impossible for me to suspect
a man of Mr. *Snake's* sensibility and discernment.

LADY SNEER. Well, well, no compliments now;—
but tell me when you saw your mistress, *Maria*—or,
110 what is more material to me, your brother.

JOS. SURF. I have not seen either since I left you;
but I can inform you that they never meet. Some of
your stories have taken a good effect on Maria.

LADY SNEER. Ah, my dear Snake! the merit of this
belongs to you. But do your brother's distresses in-
crease?

JOS. SURF. Every hour;—I am told he has had another execution in the house yesterday; in short, his
dissipation and extravagance exceed any thing I ever
120 heard of.

LADY SNEER. Poor Charles!

JOS. SURF. True, madam;—notwithstanding his vices,
one can't help feeling for him.—Aye, poor Charles!
I'm sure I wish it was in *my* power to be of any es-
sential service to him.—For the man who does not
share in the distresses of a brother, even though
merited by his own misconduct, deserves——

LADY SNEER. O lud! you are going to be moral, and
forget that you are among friends.

Jos. Surf. Egad, that's true!—I'll keep that senti- 130
ment till I see Sir Peter. However, it is certainly a
charity to rescue Maria from such a libertine, who, if
he is to be reclaimed, can be so only by a person of
your ladyship's superior accomplishments and understanding.

Snake. I believe, Lady Sneerwell, here's company
coming,—I'll go and copy the letter I mentioned to
you.—Mr. Surface, your most obedient.   *Exit* Snake.

Jos. Surf. Sir, your very devoted.—Lady Sneerwell,
I am very sorry you have put any further confidence 140
in that fellow.

Lady Sneer. Why so?

Jos. Surf. I have lately detected him in frequent
conference with old *Rowley*, who was formerly my
father's steward, and has never, you know, been a
friend of mine.

Lady Sneer. And do you think he would betray us?

Jos. Surf. Nothing more likely: take my word for't,
Lady Sneerwell, that fellow hasn't virtue enough to be
faithful even to his own villainy.—Hah! Maria! 150

Enter Maria.

Lady Sneer. Maria, my dear, how do you do?—
What's the matter?

Maria. Oh! there is that disagreeable lover of mine,
Sir *Benjamin Backbite*, has just called at my guardian's, with his odious uncle, *Crabtree*; so I slipped out,
and run hither to avoid them.

Lady Sneer. Is that all?

Jos. Surf. If my brother *Charles* had been of the
party, ma'am, perhaps you would not have been so
much alarmed. 160

Lady Sneer. Nay, now you are severe; for I dare
swear the truth of the matter is, Maria heard *you*
were here;—but, my dear, what has Sir Benjamin
done, that you should avoid him so?

Maria. Oh, he has done nothing—but 'tis for what

he has said,—his conversation is a perpetual libel on all his acquaintance.

Jos. Surf. Aye, and the worst of it is, there is no advantage in not knowing him; for he'll abuse a
170 stranger just as soon as his best friend—and his uncle's as bad.

Lady Sneer. Nay, but we should make allowance; Sir Benjamin is a wit and a poet.

Maria. For my part, I own, madam, wit loses its respect with me, when I see it in company with malice. —What do you think, Mr. Surface?

Jos. Surf. Certainly, madam; to smile at the jest which plants a thorn in another's breast is to become a principal in the mischief.

180 Lady Sneer. Pshaw! there's no possibility of being witty without a little ill nature: the malice of a good thing is the barb that makes it stick.—What's your opinion, Mr. Surface?

Jos. Surf. To be sure, madam, that conversation, where the spirit of raillery is suppressed, will ever appear tedious and insipid.

Maria. Well, I'll not debate how far scandal may be allowable; but in a man, I am sure, it is always contemptible.—We have pride, envy, rivalship, and a
190 thousand motives to depreciate each other; but the male slanderer must have the cowardice of a woman before he can traduce one.

Enter Servant.

Serv. Madam, Mrs. Candour is below, and, if your ladyship's at leisure, will leave her carriage.

Lady Sneer. Beg her to walk in. [*Exit Servant.*] Now Maria, however here is a character to your taste; for, though Mrs. Candour is a little talkative, every-body allows her to be the best-natured and best sort of woman.

200 Maria. Yes, with a very gross affectation of good

nature and benevolence, she does more mischief than the direct malice of old Crabtree.

JOS. SURF. I'faith 'tis very true, Lady Sneerwell; whenever I hear the current running against the characters of my friends, I never think them in such danger as when Candour undertakes their defence.

LADY SNEER. Hush!—here she is!

Enter MRS. CANDOUR.

MRS. CAN. My dear Lady Sneerwell, how have you been this century?—Mr. Surface, what news do you hear?—though indeed it is no matter, for I think one 210 hears nothing else but scandal.

JOS. SURF. Just so, indeed, madam.

MRS. CAN. Ah, Maria! child,—what, is the whole affair off between you and Charles? His extravagance, I presume—the town talks of nothing else.

MARIA. I am very sorry, ma'am, the town has so little to do.

MRS. CAN. True, true, child: but there is no stopping people's tongues.—I own I was hurt to hear it, as indeed I was to learn, from the same quarter, that 220 your guardian, Sir Peter, and Lady Teazle have not agreed lately so well as could be wished.

MARIA. 'Tis strangely impertinent for people to busy themselves so.

MRS. CAN. Very true, child, but what's to be done? People will talk—there's no preventing it.—Why, it was but yesterday I was told that Miss Gadabout had eloped with Sir Filigree Flirt.—But, Lord! there's no minding what one hears—though, to be sure, I had this from very good authority. 230

MARIA. Such reports are highly scandalous.

MRS. CAN. So they are, child—shameful, shameful! But the world is so censorious, no character escapes.— Lord, now who would have suspected your friend, Miss Prim, of an indiscretion? Yet such is the ill-nature of people, that they say her uncle stopped her last week, just as she was stepping into the York Diligence with her dancing-master.

MARIA. I'll answer for't there are no grounds for the 240 report.

MRS. CAN. Oh, no foundation in the world, I dare swear; no more, probably, than for the story circulated last month, of Mrs. Festino's affair with Colonel Cassino;—though, to be sure, that matter was never rightly cleared up.

JOS. SURF. The license of invention some people take is monstrous indeed.

MARIA. 'Tis so.—But, in my opinion, those who report such things are equally culpable.

250 MRS. CAN. To be sure they are; tale-bearers are as bad as the tale-makers—'tis an old observation, and a very true one—but what's to be done, as I said before? how will you prevent people from talking?—To-day, Mrs. Clackit assured me Mr. and Mrs. Honeymoon were at last become mere man and wife, like the rest of their acquaintances.—She likewise hinted that a certain widow, in the next street, had got rid of her dropsy and recovered her shape in a most surprising manner. And at the same time Miss Tattle, who was 260 by, affirmed that Lord Buffalo had discovered his lady at a house of no extraordinary fame—and that Sir Harry Bouquet and Tom Saunter were to measure swords on a similar provocation. But, Lord, do you think I would report these things! No, no! tale-bearers, as I said before, are just as bad as tale-makers.

JOS. SURF. Ah! Mrs. Candour, if everybody had your forbearance and good nature!

MRS. CAN. I confess, Mr. Surface, I cannot bear to hear people attacked behind their backs, and when 270 ugly circumstances come out against one's acquaintance I own I always love to think the best.—By the bye, I hope it is not true that your brother is absolutely ruined?

Jos. SURF. I am afraid his circumstances are very bad indeed, ma'am.

MRS. CAN. Ah!—I heard so—but you must tell him to keep up his spirits—everybody almost is in the same way! Lord Spindle, Sir Thomas Splint, Captain Quinze, and Mr. Nickit—all up, I hear, within this week; so, if Charles is undone, he'll find half his acquaintances 280 ruined too—and that, you know, is a consolation.

Jos. SURF. Doubtless, ma'am—a very great one.

Enter Servant.

SERV. Mr. Crabtree and Sir Benjamin Backbite.

Exit Servant.

LADY SNEER. So, Maria, you see your lover pursues you; positively you shan't escape.

Enter CRABTREE *and* SIR BENJAMIN BACKBITE.

CRAB. Lady Sneerwell, I kiss your hands. Mrs. Candour, I don't believe you are acquainted with my nephew, Sir Benjamin Backbite? Egad, ma'am, he has a pretty wit, and is a pretty poet too; isn't he, Lady Sneerwell? 290

SIR BEN. O fie, uncle!

CRAB. Nay, egad it's true—I'll back him at a rebus or a charade against the best rhymer in the kingdom. Has your ladyship heard the epigram he wrote last week on Lady Frizzle's feather catching fire?—Do, Benjamin, repeat it—or the charade you made last night extempore at Mrs. Drowzie's conversazione.— Come now; your *first* is the name of a fish, your *second* a great naval commander, and——

SIR BEN. Uncle, now—prithee—— 300

CRAB. I'faith, ma'am, 'twould surprise you to hear how ready he is at these things.

LADY SNEER. I wonder, Sir Benjamin, you never publish anything.

SIR BEN. To say truth, ma'am, 'tis very vulgar to print; and, as my little productions are mostly satires and lampoons on particular people, I find they circulate more by giving copies in confidence to the friends of the parties—however, I have some love
310 elegies, which, when favored with this lady's smiles, I mean to give to the public.

CRAB. 'Fore heav'n, ma'am, they'll immortalize you! —you'll be handed down to posterity like Petrarch's Laura, or Waller's Sacharissa.

SIR BEN. Yes, madam, I think you will like them, when you shall see them on a beautiful quarto page, where a neat rivulet of text shall murmur through a meadow of margin. 'Fore gad, they will be the most elegant things of their kind!
320   CRAB. But, ladies, that's true—have you heard the news?

MRS. CAN. What, sir, do you mean the report of—

CRAB. No, ma'am, that's not it.—Miss Nicely is going to be married to her own footman.

MRS. CAN. Impossible!

CRAB. Ask Sir Benjamin.

SIR. BEN. 'Tis very true, ma'am—everything is fixed, and the wedding liveries bespoke.

CRAB. Yes—and they *do* say there were pressing
330 reasons for it.

LADY SNEER. Why, I *have* heard something of this before.

MRS. CAN. It can't be—and I wonder any one should believe such a story of so prudent a lady as Miss Nicely.

SIR BEN. O lud! ma'am, that's the very reason 'twas believed at once. She has always been so *cautious* and so *reserved,* that everybody was sure there was some reason for it at bottom.
340   MRS. CAN. Why, to be sure, a tale of scandal is as fatal to the credit of a prudent lady of her stamp as

a fever is generally to those of the strongest constitutions; but there is a sort of puny, sickly reputation that is always ailing, yet will outlive the robuster characters of a hundred prudes.

SIR BEN. True, madam, there are valetudinarians in reputation as well as constitution, who, being conscious of their weak part, avoid the least breath of air, and supply their want of stamina by care and circumspection.   350

MRS. CAN. Well, but this may be all a mistake. You know, Sir Benjamin, very trifling circumstances often give rise to the most injurious tales.

CRAB. That they do, I'll be sworn, ma'am. Did you ever hear how Miss Piper came to lose her lover and her character last summer at Tunbridge?—Sir Benjamin, you remember it?

SIR BEN. Oh, to be sure!—the most whimsical circumstance—

LADY SNEER. How was it, pray?   360

CRAB. Why, one evening, at Mrs. Ponto's assembly, the conversation happened to turn on the difficulty of breeding Nova Scotia sheep in this country. Says a young lady in company, 'I have known instances of it; for Miss Letitia Piper, a first cousin of mine, had a Nova Scotia sheep that produced her twins.' 'What!' cries the old Dowager Lady Dundizzy (who you know is as deaf as a post), 'has Miss Piper had twins?' This mistake, as you may imagine, threw the whole company into a fit of laughing. However, 'twas the next 370 morning everywhere reported, and in a few days believed by the whole town, that Miss Letitia Piper had actually been brought to bed of a fine boy and a girl —and in less than a week there were people who could name the father, and the farm-house where the babies were put out to nurse!

LADY SNEER. Strange, indeed!

CRAB. Matter of fact, I assure you.—O lud! Mr.

Surface, pray is it true that your uncle, Sir Oliver, is
380 coming home?

Jos. Surf. Not that I know of, indeed, sir.

Crab. He has been in the East Indias a long time.
You can scarcely remember him, I believe.—Sad comfort, whenever he returns, to hear how your brother
has gone on!

Jos. Surf. Charles has been imprudent, sir, to be
sure; but I hope no busy people have already prejudiced Sir Oliver against him,—he may reform.

Sir Ben. To be sure he may—for my part I never
390 believed him to be so utterly void of principle as people say—and though he has lost all his friends, I am
told nobody is better spoken of by the Jews.

Crab. That's true, egad, nephew. If the old Jewry
were a ward, I believe Charles would be an alderman;
no man more popular there, 'fore gad! I hear he pays
as many annuities as the Irish tontine;[2] and that,
whenever he's sick, they have prayers for the recovery
of his health in the Synagogue.

Sir Ben. Yet no man lives in greater splendor.—
400 They tell me, when he entertains his friends, he can
sit down to dinner with a dozen of his own securities;
have a score [of] tradesmen waiting in the ante-
chamber, and an officer behind every guest's chair.

Jos. Surf. This may be entertainment to you, gentlemen, but you pay very little regard to the feelings of
a brother.

Maria. [*Aside.*] Their malice is intolerable!—Lady
Sneerwell, I must wish you a good morning—I'm not
very well.   *Exit* Maria.

410   Mrs. Can. O dear! she changes color very much!

Lady Sneer. Do, Mrs. Candour, follow her—she
may want assistance.

Mrs. Can. That I will, with all my soul, ma'am.—

²**Irish tontine** a life annuity scheme sponsored by the Irish
parliament

Poor dear girl! who knows what her situation may be!

Exit Mrs. Candour.

Lady Sneer. 'Twas nothing but that she could not bear to hear Charles reflected on, notwithstanding their difference.

Sir Ben. The young lady's *penchant* is obvious.

Crab. But, Benjamin, you mustn't give up the pursuit for that; follow her, and put her into good humor. 420 Repeat her some of your own verses.—Come, I'll assist you.

Sir Ben. Mr. Surface, I did not mean to hurt you; but depend upon't your brother is utterly undone.

(*Going.*)

Crab. O lud, aye! undone as ever man was—can't raise a guinea. (*Going.*)

Sir Ben. And everything sold, I'm told, that was movable. (*Going.*)

Crab. I have seen one that was at his house—not a thing left but some empty bottles that were over- 430 looked, and the family pictures, which I believe are framed in the wainscot. (*Going.*)

Sir Ben. And I am very sorry to hear also some bad stories against him. (*Going.*)

Crab. Oh, he has done many mean things, that's certain. (*Going.*)

Sir Ben. But, however, as he's your brother—

(*Going.*)

Crab. We'll tell you all, another opportunity.

Exeunt Crabtree *and* Sir Benjamin.

Lady Sneer. Ha, ha! ha! 'tis very hard for them to leave a subject they have not quite run down. 440

Jos. Surf. And I believe the abuse was no more acceptable to your ladyship than to Maria.

Lady Sneer. I doubt[3] her affections are farther en-

---
[3] doubt fear

gaged than we imagined; but the family are to be here this evening, so you may as well dine where you are, and we shall have an opportunity of observing farther;—in the meantime, I'll go and plot mischief, and you shall study sentiments.   *Exeunt.*

SCENE II

SIR PETER TEAZLE'S *house.*

Enter SIR PETER.

SIR PETER. When an old bachelor takes a young wife, what is he to expect?—'Tis now six months since Lady Teazle made me the happiest of men—and I have been the miserablest dog ever since that ever committed wedlock! We tift a little going to church, and came to a quarrel before the bells were done ringing. I was more than once nearly choked with gall during the honeymoon, and had lost all comfort in life before my friends had done wishing me joy! Yet I
10 chose with caution—a girl bred wholly in the country, who never knew luxury beyond one silk gown, nor dissipation above the annual gala of a race ball. Yet now she plays her part in all the extravagant fopperies of the fashion and the town, with as ready a grace as if she had never seen a bush nor a grass-plat out of Grosvenor Square! I am sneered at by my old acquaintance—paragraphed in the newspapers. She dissipates my fortune, and contradicts all my humors; yet the worst of it is, I doubt I love her, or I should
20 never bear all this. However, I'll never be weak enough to own it.

Enter ROWLEY.

Row. Oh! Sir Peter, your servant,—how is it with you, sir?

SIR PET. Very bad, Master Rowley, very bad;—I meet with nothing but crosses and vexations.

Row. What can have happened to trouble you since yesterday?

Sir Pet. A good question to a married man!

Row. Nay, I'm sure your lady, Sir Peter, can't be the cause of your uneasiness. 30

Sir Pet. Why, has anyone told you she was dead?

Row. Come, come, Sir Peter, you love her, notwithstanding your tempers don't exactly agree.

Sir Pet. But the fault is entirely hers, Master Rowley. I am, myself, the sweetest-tempered man alive, and hate a teasing temper—and so I tell her a hundred times a day.

Row. Indeed!

Sir Pet. Aye; and what is very extraordinary, in all our disputes she is always in the wrong! But Lady 40 Sneerwell, and the set she meets at her house, encourage the perverseness of her disposition. Then, to complete my vexations, Maria, my ward, whom I ought to have the power of a father over, is determined to turn rebel too, and absolutely refuses the man whom I have long resolved on for her husband; —meaning, I suppose, to bestow herself on his profligate brother.

Row. You know, Sir Peter, I have always taken the liberty to differ with you on the subject of these two 50 young gentlemen. I only wish you may not be deceived in your opinion of the elder. For Charles, my life on't! he will retrieve his errors yet. Their worthy father, once my honored master, was, at his years, nearly as wild a spark; yet, when he died, he did not leave a more benevolent heart to lament his loss.

Sir Pet. You are wrong, Master Rowley. On their father's death, you know, I acted as a kind of guardian to them both, till their uncle Sir Oliver's Eastern liberality gave them an early independence; of course, 60 no person could have more opportunities of judging of their hearts, and I was never mistaken in my life. Joseph is indeed a model for the young men of the

age. He is a man of sentiment, and acts up to the
sentiments he professes; but, for the other, take my
word for't, if he had any grains of virtue by descent,
he has dissipated them with the rest of his inheritance.
Ah! my old friend, Sir Oliver, will be deeply mortified
when he finds how part of his bounty has been mis-
70   applied.

Row. I am sorry to find you so violent against the
young man, because this may be the most critical
period of his fortune. I came hither with news that will
surprise you.

Sir Pet. What! let me hear.

Row. Sir Oliver *is* arrived, and at this moment in
town.

Sir Pet. How! you astonish me! I thought you did
not expect him this month.

80   Row. I did not; but his passage has been remarkably
quick.

Sir Pet. Egad, I shall rejoice to see my old friend,
—'tis sixteen years since we met—we have had many
a day together; but does he still enjoin us not to inform his nephews of his arrival?

Row. Most strictly. He means, before it is known,
to make some trial of their dispositions.

Sir Pet. Ah! There needs no art to discover their
merits—however, he shall have his way; but, pray,
90   does he know I am married?

Row. Yes, and will soon wish you joy.

Sir Pet. What, as we drink health to a friend in a
consumption! Ah, Oliver will laugh at me— we used
to rail at matrimony together—but he has been steady
to his text. Well, he must be at my house, though—
I'll instantly give orders for his reception. But, Master
Rowley, don't drop a word that Lady Teazle and I
ever disagree.

Row. By no means.

100   Sir Pet. For I should never be able to stand Noll's

jokes; so I'd have him think, Lord forgive me! that we are a very happy couple.

Row. I understand you—but then you must be very careful not to differ while he's in the house with you.

Sir Pet. Egad, and so we must—and that's impossible. Ah! Master Rowley, when an old bachelor marries a young wife, he deserves—no—the crime carries the punishment along with it.   *Exeunt.*

End of Act Ist.

Act II

Scene I

Sir Peter Teazle's *house.*

Enter Sir Peter *and* Lady Teazle.

Sir Pet. Lady Teazle, Lady Teazle, I'll not bear it!

Lady Teaz. Sir Peter, Sir Peter, you may bear it or not, as you please; but I ought to have my own way in everything, and what's more, I *will* too.—What! though I was educated in the country, I know very well that women of fashion in London are accountable to nobody after they are married.

Sir Pet. Very well, ma'am, very well,—so a husband is to have no influence, no authority?

Lady Teaz. Authority! No, to be sure—if you 10 wanted authority over me, you should have adopted me, and not married me; I am sure you were old enough.

Sir Pet. Old enough!—aye, there it is!—Well, well, Lady Teazle, though my life may be made unhappy by your temper, I'll not be ruined by your extravagance.

LADY TEAZ. My extravagance! I'm sure I'm not more extravagant than a woman of fashion ought to be.

20   SIR PET. No, no, madam, you shall throw away no more sums on such unmeaning luxury. 'Slife! to spend as much to furnish your dressing-room with flowers in winter as would suffice to turn the Pantheon[1] into a greenhouse, and give a *fête champêtre*[2] at Christmas!

LADY TEAZ. Lord, Sir Peter, am I to blame because flowers are dear in cold weather? You should find fault with the climate, and not with me. For my part, I am sure I wish it was spring all the year round, and that roses grew under one's feet!

30   SIR PET. Oons! madam—if you had been born to this, I shouldn't wonder at your talking thus.—But you forget what your situation was when I married you.

LADY TEAZ. No, no, I don't; 'twas a very disagreeable one, or I should never have married *you*.

SIR PET. Yes, yes, madam, you were then in somewhat an humbler style—the daughter of a plain country squire. Recollect, Lady Teazle, when I saw you first, sitting at your tambour,[3] in a pretty figured linen
40   gown, with a bunch of keys by your side, your hair combed smooth over a roll, and your apartment hung round with fruits in worsted, of your own working.

LADY TEAZ. O, yes! I remember it very well, and a curious life I led—my daily occupation to inspect the dairy, superintend the poultry, make extracts from the family receipt-book, and comb my aunt Deborah's lapdog.

SIR PET. Yes, yes, ma'am, 'twas so indeed.

LADY TEAZ. And then, you know, my evening amuse-

---

[1] **the Pantheon** a large concert hall in London, so called because it had a dome like that of the Pantheon in Rome   [2] **fête champêtre** outdoor entertainment   [3] **tambour** a circular frame used for embroidering

ments! To draw patterns for ruffles, which I had not 50
the materials to make; to play Pope Joan[4] with the
curate; to read a novel to my aunt; or to be stuck down
to an old spinet to strum my father to sleep after a
fox-chase.

SIR PET. I am glad you have so good a memory.
Yes, madam, these were the recreations I took you
from; but now you must have your coach—*vis-à-vis*—
and three powdered footmen before your chair and,
in summer, a pair of white cats[5] to draw you to Ken-
sington Gardens.—No recollection, I suppose, when 60
you were content to ride double, behind the butler,
on a docked coach-horse?

LADY TEAZ. No—I swear I never did that—I deny
the butler and the coach-horse.

SIR PET. This, madam, was your situation—and
what have I not done for you? I have made you a
woman of fashion, of fortune, of rank—in short, I
have made you my wife.

LADY TEAZ. Well, then, and there is but one thing
more you can make me to add to the obligation—and 70
that is——

SIR PET. My widow, I suppose?

LADY TEAZ. Hem! hem!

SIR PET. Thank you, madam—but don't flatter yourself; for though your ill-conduct may disturb my
peace, it shall never break my heart, I promise you:
however, I am equally obliged to you for the hint.

LADY TEAZ. Then why will you endeavor to make
yourself so disagreeable to me, and thwart me in every
little elegant expense?   80

SIR PET. 'Slife, madam, I say, had you any of these
elegant expenses when you married me?

LADY TEAZ. Lud, Sir Peter! would you have me be
out of the fashion?

SIR PET. The fashion, indeed! what had you to do
with the fashion before you married me?

[4] **Pope Joan** a card game   [5] **cats** horses

LADY TEAZ. For my part, I should think you would like to have your wife thought a woman of taste.

SIR PET. Aye—there again—taste! Zounds! madam, 90 you had no taste when you married *me!*

LADY TEAZ. That's very true, indeed, Sir Peter! and, *after* having married you, I am sure I should never pretend to taste again! But now, Sir Peter, if we have finished our daily jangle, I presume I may go to my engagement of [at] Lady Sneerwell's?

SIR PET. Aye—there's another precious circumstance!—a charming set of acquaintance you have made there!

LADY TEAZ. Nay, Sir Peter, they are people of rank 100 and fortune, and remarkably tenacious of reputation.

SIR PET. Yes, egad, they are tenacious of reputation with a vengeance; for they don't choose anybody should have a character but themselves! Such a crew! Ah! many a wretch has rid on a hurdle[6] who has done less mischief than those utterers of forged tales, coiners of scandal,—and clippers of reputation.

LADY TEAZ. What! would you restrain the freedom of speech?

SIR PET. Oh! they have made you just as bad as any 110 one of the society.

LADY TEAZ. Why, I believe I do bear a part with a tolerable grace. But I vow I have no malice against the people I abuse; when I say an ill-natured thing, 'tis out of pure good humor—and I take it for granted they deal exactly in the same manner with me. But, Sir Peter, you know you promised to come to Lady Sneerwell's too.

SIR PET. Well, well, I'll call in just to look after my own character.

120 LADY TEAZ. Then, indeed, you must make haste after me or you'll be too late.—So good-bye to ye.

Exit LADY TEAZLE.

[6] **hurdle** sledge on which traitors were taken to the place of execution

SIR PET. So—I have gained much by my intended expostulations! Yet with what a charming air she contradicts everything I say, and how pleasingly she shows her contempt of my authority. Well, though I can't make her love me, there is a great satisfaction in quarreling with her; and I think she never appears to such advantage as when she's doing everything in her power to plague me.   *Exit.*

SCENE II

LADY SNEERWELL'S.

LADY SNEERWELL, MRS. CANDOUR, CRABTREE, SIR BENJAMIN BACKBITE, *and* JOSEPH SURFACE.

LADY SNEER. Nay, positively, we will hear it.

JOS. SURF. Yes, yes, the epigram, by all means.

SIR BEN. Plague on't, uncle! 'tis mere nonsense.

CRAB. No, no; 'fore gad, very clever for an extempore!

SIR BEN. But, ladies, you should be acquainted with the circumstance,—you must know, that one day last week, as Lady Betty Curricle was taking the dust in Hyde Park, in a sort of duodecimo[7] phaëton, she desired me to write some verses on her ponies; upon 10 which, I took out my pocket-book, and in one moment produced the following:

'Sure never were seen two such beautiful ponies!
Other horses are clowns, and these macaronies!
Nay, to give 'em this title I'm sure isn't wrong—
Their legs are so slim, and their tails are so long.'

CRAB. There, ladies—done in the smack of a whip, and on horseback too!

[7] **duodecimo** very small (a bibliographical term)

Jos. Surf. A very Phœbus, mounted—indeed, Sir
20 Benjamin.

Sir Ben. O dear sir—trifles—trifles.

Enter Lady Teazle *and* Maria.

Mrs. Can. I must have a copy.

Lady Sneer. Lady Teazle, I hope we shall see Sir
Peter.

Lady Teaz. I believe he'll wait on your ladyship
presently.

Lady Sneer. Maria, my love, you look grave. Come,
you shall sit down to cards with Mr. Surface.

Maria. I take very little pleasure in cards—how-
30 ever, I'll do as your ladyship pleases.

Lady Teaz. [*Aside.*] I am surprised Mr. Surface
should sit down with *her.*—I thought he would have
embraced this opportunity of speaking to me before
Sir Peter came.

Mrs. Can. Now, I'll die but you are so scandalous,
I'll forswear your society.

Lady Teaz. What's the matter, Mrs. Candour?

Mrs. Can. They'll not allow our friend Miss Ver-
milion to be handsome.

40 Lady Sneer. Oh, surely, she's a pretty woman.

Crab. I am very glad you think so, ma'am.

Mrs. Can. She has a charming fresh color.

Lady Teaz. Yes, when it is fresh put on.

Mrs. Can. O fie! I'll swear her color is natural—I
have seen it come and go.

Lady Teaz. I dare swear you have, ma'am—it goes
of a night, and comes again in the morning.

Mrs. Can. Ha! ha! ha! how I hate to hear you talk
so! But surely, now, her sister *is,* or *was,* very hand-
50 some.

Crab. Who? Mrs. Evergreen?—O Lord! she's six-
and-fifty if she's an hour!

Mrs. Can. Now positively you wrong her; fifty-two

or fifty-three is the utmost—and I don't think she looks more.

SIR BEN. Ah! there is no judging by her looks, unless one could see her face.

LADY SNEER. Well, well, if Mrs. Evergreen *does* take some pains to repair the ravages of time, you must allow she effects it with great ingenuity; and 60 surely that's better than the careless manner in which the widow Ochre caulks her wrinkles.

SIR BEN. Nay, now, Lady Sneerwell, you are severe upon the widow. Come, come, it is not that she paints so ill—but, when she has finished her face, she joins it on so badly to her neck, that she looks like a mended statue, in which the connoisseur may see at once that the head's modern, though the trunk's antique!

CRAB. Ha! ha! ha! Well said, nephew!

MRS. CAN. Ha! ha! ha! Well, you make me laugh, 70 but I vow I hate you for't.—What do you think of Miss Simper?

SIR BEN. Why, she has very pretty teeth.

LADY TEAZ. Yes; and on that account, when she is neither speaking nor laughing (which very seldom happens), she never absolutely shuts her mouth, but leaves it always on a jar, as it were.

MRS. CAN. How can you be so ill-natured?

LADY TEAZ. Nay, I allow even that's better than the pains Mrs. Prim takes to conceal her losses in front. 80 She draws her mouth till it positively resembles the aperture of a poor's-box, and all her words appear to slide out edgeways.

LADY SNEER. Very well, Lady Teazle; I see you can be a little severe.

LADY TEAZ. In defence of a friend it is but justice; —but here comes Sir Peter to spoil our pleasantry.

Enter SIR PETER TEAZLE.

SIR PET. Ladies, your most obedient—Mercy on me,

here is the whole set! a character dead at every word,
90 I suppose.   (*Aside.*)

MRS. CAN. I am rejoiced you are come, Sir Peter.
They have been *so* censorious. They will allow good
qualities to nobody—not even good nature to our
friend Mrs. Pursy.

LADY TEAZ. What, the fat dowager who was at Mrs.
Codille's last night?

MRS. CAN. Nay, her bulk is her misfortune; and,
when she takes such pains to get rid of it, you ought
not to reflect on her.

100 LADY SNEER. That's very true, indeed.

LADY TEAZ. Yes, I know she almost lives on acids
and small whey; laces herself by pulleys; and often, in
the hottest noon of summer, you may see her on a
little squat pony, with her hair platted up behind like
a drummer's, and puffing round the Ring[8] on a full
trot.

MRS. CAN. I thank you, Lady Teazle, for defending
her.

SIR PET. Yes, a good defence, truly.

110 MRS. CAN. But Sir Benjamin is as censorious as Miss
Sallow.

CRAB. Yes, and she is a curious being to pretend to
be censorious!—an awkward gawky, without any one
good point under heaven.

MRS. CAN. Positively you shall not be so very severe.
Miss Sallow is a relation of mine by marriage, and,
as for her person, great allowance is to be made; for,
let me tell you, a woman labors under many disad-
vantages who tries to pass for a girl at six-and-thirty.

120 LADY SNEER. Though, surely, she is handsome still
—and for the weakness in her eyes, considering how
much she reads by candle-light, it is not to be won-
dered at.

MRS. CAN. True; and then as to her manner, upon
my word I think it is particularly graceful, considering

[8] **Ring** a drive and promenade in Hyde Park

she never had the least education; for you know her mother was a Welch milliner, and her father a sugar-baker at Bristol.

SIR BEN. Ah! you are both of you too good-natured!

SIR PET. Yes, damned good-natured! This their own 130 relation! mercy on me!   (*Aside.*)

SIR BEN. And Mrs. Candour is of so moral a turn she can sit for an hour to hear Lady Stucco talk sentiment.

LADY TEAZ. Nay, I vow Lady Stucco is very well with the dessert after dinner; for she's just like the French fruit one cracks for mottoes—made up of paint and proverb.

MRS. CAN. Well, I never will join in ridiculing a friend; and so I constantly tell my cousin Ogle, and 140 you all know what pretensions she has to be critical in beauty.

CRAB. Oh, to be sure! she has herself the oddest countenance that ever was seen; 'tis a collection of features from all the different countries of the globe.

SIR BEN. So she has, indeed—an Irish front!

CRAB. Caledonian locks!

SIR BEN. Dutch nose!

CRAB. Austrian lip!

SIR BEN. Complexion of a Spaniard!   150

CRAB. And teeth *à la Chinoise!*

SIR BEN. In short, her face resembles a *table d'hôte* at Spa—where no two guests are of a nation——

CRAB. Or a congress at the close of a general war —wherein all the members, even to her eyes, appear to have a different interest, and her nose and chin are the only parties likely to join issue.

MRS. CAN. Ha! ha! ha!

SIR PET. Mercy on my life!—a person they dine with twice a week!   (*Aside.*) 160

[LADY SNEER. Go—go—you are a couple of provoking toads.]

MRS. CAN. Nay, but I vow you shall not carry

the laugh off so—for give me leave to say, that Mrs. Ogle—

SIR PET. Madam, madam, I beg your pardon—there's no stopping these good gentlemen's tongues. But when I tell *you*, Mrs. Candour, that the lady they are abusing is a particular friend of mine—I hope 170 you'll not take her part.

LADY SNEER. Well said, Sir Peter! but you are a cruel creature—too phlegmatic yourself for a jest, and too peevish to allow wit on others.

SIR PET. Ah, madam, true wit is more nearly allied to good nature than your ladyship is aware of.

LADY TEAZ. True, Sir Peter; I believe they are so near akin that they can never be united.

SIR BEN. Or rather, madam, suppose them man and wife, because one so seldom sees them together.

180 LADY TEAZ. But Sir Peter is such an enemy to scandal, I believe he would have it put down by parliament.

SIR PET. 'Fore heaven, madam, if they were to consider the sporting with reputation of as much importance as poaching on manors, and pass *An Act for the Preservation of Fame,* I believe many would thank them for the bill.

LADY SNEER. O lud! Sir Peter; would you deprive us of our privileges?

190 SIR PET. Aye, madam; and then no person should be permitted to kill characters or run down reputations, but qualified old maids and disappointed widows.

LADY SNEER. Go, you monster!

MRS. CAN. But sure you would not be quite so severe on those who only report what they hear.

SIR PET. Yes, madam, I would have law merchant[9] for them too; and in all cases of slander currency, whenever the drawer of the lie was not to be found,

[9] **law merchant** system of laws for the regulation of commerce

the injured parties should have a right to come on any 200
of the indorsers.

CRAB. Well, for my part, I believe there never was
a scandalous tale without some foundation.

LADY SNEER. Come, ladies, shall we sit down to
cards in the next room?

Enter Servant and whispers SIR PETER.

SIR PET. I'll be with them directly.—[*Exit Servant.*]
I'll get away unperceived. [*Aside.*]

LADY SNEER. Sir Peter, you are not leaving us?

SIR PET. Your ladyship must excuse me; I'm called
away by particular business—but I leave my charac- 210
ter behind me.   *Exit* SIR PETER.

SIR BEN. Well certainly, Lady Teazle, that lord of
yours is a strange being; I could tell you some stories
of him would make you laugh heartily, if he wasn't
your husband.

LADY TEAZ. O pray don't mind that—come, do let's
hear them.

(*They join the rest of the company, all talking
as they are going into the next room.*)

JOS. SURF. (*Rising with* MARIA.) Maria, I see you
have no satisfaction in this society.

MARIA. How is it possible I should? If to raise 220
malicious smiles at the infirmities and misfortunes of
those who have never injured us be the province of
wit or humor, heaven grant me a double portion of
dulness!

JOS. SURF. Yet they appear more ill-natured than
they are; they have no malice at heart.

MARIA. Then is their conduct still more contemptible; for, in my opinion, nothing could excuse the
intemperance of their tongues but a natural and un-
governable bitterness of mind.   230

JOS. SURF. But can you, Maria, feel thus for others,

and be unkind to me alone? Is hope to be denied the tenderest passion?

MARIA. Why will you distress me by renewing this subject?

JOS. SURF. Ah, Maria! you would not treat me thus, and oppose your guardian, Sir Peter's will, but that I see that profligate *Charles* is still a favored rival.

240 MARIA. Ungenerously urged! But, whatever my sentiments of that unfortunate young man are, be assured I shall not feel more bound to give him up, because his distresses have lost him the regard even of a brother.

(LADY TEAZLE *returns.*)

JOS. SURF. Nay, but, Maria, do not leave me with a frown—by all that's honest, I swear—Gad's life, here's Lady Teazle. (*Aside.*)—You must not—no, you shall not—for, though I have the greatest regard for Lady Teazle——

MARIA. Lady Teazle!

250 JOS. SURF. Yet were Sir Peter to suspect——

LADY TEAZ. (*Coming forward.*) What's this, pray? Do you take her for me?—Child, you are wanted in the next room.—   *Exit* MARIA.
What is all this, pray?

JOS. SURF. Oh, the most unlucky circumstance in nature! Maria has somehow suspected the tender concern I have for your happiness, and threatened to acquaint Sir Peter with her suspicions, and I was just endeavoring to reason with her when you came.

260 LADY TEAZ. Indeed! but you seemed to adopt a very tender mode of reasoning—do you *usually* argue on your knees?

JOS. SURF. Oh, she's a child—and I thought a little bombast——but, Lady Teazle, when are you to give me your judgment on my library, as you promised?

LADY TEAZ. No, no,—I begin to think it would be

imprudent, and you know I admit you as a lover no
further than *fashion* requires.

Jos. Surf. True—a mere Platonic cicisbeo,[10] what
every London wife is *entitled* to.   270

Lady Teaz. Certainly, one must not be out of the
fashion; however, I have so many of my country prejudices left, that, though Sir Peter's ill humor may vex
me ever so, it never shall provoke me to——

Jos. Surf. The only revenge in your power. Well,
I applaud your moderation.

Lady Teaz. Go—you are an insinuating wretch!
But we shall be missed—let us join the company.

Jos. Surf. But we had best not return together.

Lady Teaz. Well, don't stay—for Maria shan't come 280
to hear any more of your *reasoning*, I promise you.

                              Exit Lady Teazle.

Jos. Surf. A curious dilemma, truly, my politics have
run me into! I wanted, at first, only to ingratiate myself with Lady Teazle, that she might not be my
enemy with Maria; and I have, I don't know how, become her serious lover. Sincerely I begin to wish I had
never made such a point of gaining so *very good* a
character, for it has led me into so many cursed
rogueries that I doubt I shall be exposed at last. *Exit.*

Scene III

Sir Peter's.

Enter Sir Oliver Surface *and* Rowley.

Sir Oliv. Ha! ha! ha! and so my old friend is married, hey?—a young wife out of the country.— Ha!
ha! ha!—that he should have stood bluff [11] to old
bachelor so long, and sink into a husband at last!

---

[10] **cicisbeo** recognized gallant of a married woman   [11] **bluff** firm

Row. But you must not rally him on the subject, Sir Oliver; 'tis a tender point, I assure you, though he has been married only seven months.

Sir Oliv. Then he has been just half a year on the stool of repentance!—Poor Peter! But you say he has 10 entirely given up Charles—never sees him, hey?

Row. His prejudice against him is astonishing, and I am sure greatly increased by a jealousy of him with Lady Teazle, which he has been industriously led into by a scandalous society in the neighborhood, who have contributed not a little to Charles's ill name; whereas the truth is, I believe, if the lady is partial to either of them, his brother is the favorite.

Sir Oliv. Aye,—I know there are a set of malicious, prating, prudent gossips, both male and female, who 20 murder characters to kill time, and will rob a young fellow of his good name before he has years to know the value of it,—but I am not to be prejudiced against my nephew by such, I promise you! No, no;—if Charles has done nothing false or mean, I shall compound for his extravagance.

Row. Then, my life on't, you will reclaim him.— Ah, sir, it gives me new life to find that *your* heart is not turned against him, and that the son of my good old master has one friend, however, left.

30 Sir Oliv. What! shall I forget, Master Rowley, when I was at his years myself? Egad, my brother and I were neither of us very *prudent* youths—and yet, I believe, you have not seen many better men than your old master was?

Row. Sir, 'tis this reflection gives me assurance that Charles may yet be a credit to his family.—But here comes Sir Peter.

Sir Oliv. Egad, so he does!—Mercy on me, he's greatly altered, and seems to have a settled married 40 look! One may read husband in his face at this distance!

Enter Sir Peter Teazle.

Sir Pet. Hah! Sir Oliver—my old friend! Welcome to England a thousand times!

Sir Oliv. Thank you, thank you, Sir Peter! and i'faith I am glad to find you well, believe me!

Sir Pet. Ah! 'tis a long time since we met—sixteen years, I doubt, Sir Oliver, and many a cross accident in the time.

Sir Oliv. Aye, I have had my share—but, what! I find you are married, hey, my old boy?—Well, well, 50 it can't be helped—and so I wish you joy with all my heart!

Sir Pet. Thank you, thank you, Sir Oliver.—Yes, I have entered into the happy state—but we'll not talk of that now.

Sir Oliv. True, true, Sir Peter; old friends should not begin on grievances at first meeting. No, no, no.

Row. (*to* Sir Oliver.) Take care, pray, sir.

Sir Oliv. Well, so one of my nephews is a wild rogue, hey? 60

Sir Pet. Wild! Ah! my old friend, I grieve for your disappointment there—he's a lost young man, indeed; however, his brother will make you amends; *Joseph* is, indeed, what a youth should be—everybody in the world speaks well of him.

Sir Oliv. I am sorry to hear it—he has too good a character to be an honest fellow.—Everybody speaks well of him! Psha! then he has bowed as low to knaves and fools as to the honest dignity of genius or virtue.

Sir Pet. What, Sir Oliver! do you blame him for 70 not making enemies?

Sir Oliv. Yes, if he has merit enough to deserve them.

Sir Pet. Well, well—you'll be convinced when you know him. 'Tis edification to hear him converse—he professes the noblest sentiments.

Sir Oliv. Ah, plague of his sentiments! If he salutes

me with a scrap of morality in his mouth, I shall be
sick directly. But, however, don't mistake me, Sir
80 Peter; I don't mean to defend Charles's errors—but,
before I form my judgment of either of them, I intend
to make a trial of their hearts—and my friend Rowley
and I have planned something for the purpose.

Row. And Sir Peter shall own for once he has been
mistaken.

Sir Pet. Oh, my life on Joseph's honor!

Sir Oliv. Well, come, give us a bottle of good wine,
and we'll drink the lad's health, and tell you our
scheme.

90   Sir Pet. *Allons,* then!

Sir Oliv. And don't, Sir Peter, be so severe against
your old friend's son. Odds my life! I am not sorry
that he has run out of the course a little; for my part,
I hate to see prudence clinging to the green succors
of youth; 'tis like ivy round a sapling, and spoils the
growth of the tree.   *Exeunt.*

End of Act the Second.

Act III

Scene I

Sir Peter's.

Sir Peter Teazle, Sir Oliver Surface, *and* Rowley.

Sir Pet. Well, then—we will see this fellow first,
and have our wine afterwards. But how is this, Master
Rowley? I don't see the jet[1] of your scheme.

Row. Why, sir, this Mr. Stanley, whom I was speak-

---

[1] jet point

ing of, is nearly related to them, by their mother; he was once a merchant in Dublin, but has been ruined by a series of undeserved misfortunes. He has applied, by letter, since his confinement, both to Mr. *Surface* and *Charles*—from the former he has received nothing but evasive promises of future service, while Charles 10 has done all that his extravagance has left him power to do; and he is, at this time, endeavoring to raise a sum of money, part of which, in the midst of his own distresses, I know he intends for the service of poor Stanley.

Sir Oliv. Ah! he is my brother's son.

Sir Pet. Well, but how is Sir Oliver personally to——

Row. Why, sir, I will inform Charles and his brother that Stanley has obtained permission to apply in per- 20 son to his friends, and, as they have neither of them ever seen him, let Sir Oliver assume his character, and he will have a fair opportunity of judging at least of the benevolence of their dispositions; and believe me, sir, you will find in the youngest brother one who, in the midst of folly and dissipation, has still, as our immortal bard expresses it,—

> 'a tear for pity, and a hand
> Open as day, for melting charity.'[2]

Sir Pet. Psha! What signifies his having an open 30 hand or purse either, when he has nothing left to give? Well, well, make the trial, if you please; but where is the fellow whom you brought for Sir Oliver to examine, relative to Charles's affairs?

Row. Below, waiting his commands, and no one can give him better intelligence.—This, Sir Oliver, is a friendly Jew, who, to do him justice, has done everything in his power to bring your nephew to a proper sense of his extravagance.

Sir Pet. Pray let us have him in.   40

---

[2] 'a tear . . . charity.' *Henry IV, Part II*, IV.iv.31-32

Row. Desire Mr. Moses to walk upstairs.

Sir Pet. But why should you suppose he will speak the truth?

Row. Oh, I have convinced him that he has no chance of recovering certain sums advanced to Charles but through the bounty of Sir Oliver, who he knows is arrived; so that you may depend on his fidelity to his [own] interest. I have also another evidence in my power, one Snake, whom I have detected in a
50 matter little short of forgery, and shall shortly produce to remove some of *your* prejudices, Sir Peter, relative to Charles and Lady Teazle.

Sir Pet. I have heard too much on that subject.

Row. Here comes the honest Israelite.

Enter Moses.

—This is Sir Oliver.

Sir Oliv. Sir, I understand you have lately had great dealings with my nephew Charles.

Mos. Yes, Sir Oliver—I have done all I could for him, but he was ruined before he came to me for as-
60 sistance.

Sir Oliv. That was unlucky, truly—for you have had no opportunity of showing your talents.

Mos. None at all—I hadn't the pleasure of knowing his distresses—till he was some thousands worse than nothing.

Sir Oliv. Unfortunate, indeed! But I suppose you have done all in your power for him, honest Moses?

Mos. Yes, he knows that. This very evening I was to have brought him a gentleman from the City, who
70 doesn't know him, and will, I believe, advance him some money.

Sir Pet. What, one Charles has never had money from before?

Mos. Yes; Mr. Premium, of Crutched Friars[3]—formerly a broker.

³ **Crutched Friars** street near the Tower of London

Sir Pet. Egad, Sir Oliver, a thought strikes me!—
Charles, you say, doesn't know Mr. Premium?

Mos. Not at all.

Sir Pet. Now then, Sir Oliver, you may have a better opportunity of satisfying yourself than by an old 80
romancing tale of a poor relation;—go with my friend
Moses, and represent Mr. *Premium,* and then, I'll answer for't, you will see your nephew in all his glory.

Sir Oliv. Egad, I like this idea better than the other,
and I may visit *Joseph* afterwards, as old *Stanley.*

Sir Pet. True—so you may.

Row. Well, this is taking Charles rather at a dis-
advantage, to be sure. However, Moses—you understand Sir Peter, and will be faithful?

Mos. You may depend upon me,—this is near the 90
time I was to have gone.

Sir Oliv. I'll accompany you as soon as you please,
Moses; but hold! I have forgot one thing—how the
plague shall I be able to pass for a Jew?

Mos. There's no need—the principal is Christian.

Sir Oliv. Is he?—I'm sorry to hear it—but, then
again, an't I rather too smartly dressed to look like a
money-lender?

Sir Pet. Not at all; 'twould not be out of character,
if you went in your own carriage—would it, Moses? 100

Mos. Not in the least.

Sir Oliv. Well, but how must I talk? there's certainly some cant of usury, and mode of treating, that
I ought to know.

Sir Pet. Oh, there's not much to learn—the great
point, as I take it, is to be exorbitant enough in your
demands—hey, Moses?

Mos. Yes, that's a very great point.

Sir Oliv. I'll answer for't I'll not be wanting in
that. I'll ask him eight or ten per cent on the loan, 110
at least.

Mos. If you ask him no more than that, you'll be
discovered immediately.

Sir Oliv. Hey! what the plague! how much then?

Mos. That depends upon the circumstances. If he appears not very anxious for the supply, you should require only forty or fifty per cent; but if you find him in great distress, and want the moneys very bad—you may ask double.

120   Sir Pet. A good honest trade you're learning, Sir Oliver!

Sir Oliv. Truly I think so—and not unprofitable.

Mos. Then, you know, you haven't the moneys yourself, but are forced to borrow them for him of a friend.

Sir Oliv. Oh! I borrow it of a friend, do I?

Mos. Yes, and your friend is an unconscionable dog, but you can't help it.

Sir Oliv. My friend is an unconscionable dog, is he?

Mos. Yes, and he himself has not the moneys by 130 him—but is forced to sell stock at a great loss.

Sir Oliv. He is forced to sell stock, is he, at a great loss, is he? Well, that's very kind of him.

Sir Pet. I'faith, Sir Oliver—Mr. Premium, I mean—you'll soon be master of the trade. But, Moses! wouldn't you have him run out a little against the Annuity Bill? [4] That would be in character, I should think.

Mos. Very much.

Row. And lament that a young man now must be 140 at years of discretion before he is suffered to ruin himself?

Mos. Aye, great pity!

Sir Pet. And abuse the public for allowing merit to an act whose only object is to snatch misfortune and imprudence from the rapacious relief of usury, and give the minor a chance of inheriting his estate without being undone by coming into possession.

Sir Oliv. So, so—Moses shall give me further instructions as we go together.

[4] **Annuity Bill** measure to protect the estates of minors which became law during the initial run of the play

Sɪʀ Pᴇᴛ. You will not have much time, for your 150
nephew lives hard by.

Sɪʀ Oʟɪv. Oh, never fear! my tutor appears so able,
that though Charles lived in the next street, it must be
my own fault if I am not a complete rogue before I
turn the corner.   *Exeunt* Sɪʀ Oʟɪᴠᴇʀ *and* Mᴏsᴇs.

Sɪʀ Pᴇᴛ. So now I think Sir Oliver will be convinced;—you are partial, Rowley, and would have pre-
pared Charles for the other plot.

Row. No, upon my word, Sir Peter.

Sɪʀ Pᴇᴛ. Well, go bring me this Snake, and I'll hear 160
what he has to say presently.—I see Maria, and want
to speak with her.—*Exit* Rᴏᴡʟᴇʏ. I should be glad
to be convinced my suspicions of Lady Teazle and
Charles were unjust. I have never yet opened my
mind on this subject to my friend *Joseph*—I'm determined I will do it—*he* will give me his opinion sincerely.

Enter Mᴀʀɪᴀ.

So, child, has Mr. Surface returned with you?

Mᴀʀɪᴀ. No, sir—he was engaged.

Sɪʀ Pᴇᴛ. Well, Maria, do you not reflect, the more 170
you converse with that amiable young man, what return his partiality for you deserves?

Mᴀʀɪᴀ. Indeed, Sir Peter, your frequent impor-
tunity on this subject distresses me extremely—you
compel me to declare, that I know no man who has
ever paid me a particular attention whom I would
not prefer to Mr. Surface.

Sɪʀ Pᴇᴛ. So—here's perverseness! No, no, Maria,
'tis Charles only whom you would prefer—'tis evident
his vices and follies have won your heart.   180

Mᴀʀɪᴀ. This is unkind, sir—you know I have
obeyed you in neither seeing nor corresponding with
him; I have heard enough to convince me that he is
unworthy my regard. Yet I cannot think it culpable,

if, while my understanding severely condemns his
vices, my heart suggests some pity for his distresses.

SIR PET. Well, well, pity him as much as you please,
but give your heart and hand to a worthier object.

MARIA. Never to his brother!

190   SIR PET. Go, perverse and obstinate! But take care,
madam; you have never yet known what the authority
of a guardian is—don't compel me to inform you of it.

MARIA. I can only say, you shall not have *just* reason.
'Tis true, by my father's will, I am for a short period
bound to regard you as his substitute, but must cease
to think you so, when you would compel me to be
miserable.   *Exit* MARIA.

SIR PET. Was ever man so crossed as I am! everything conspiring to fret me!—I had not been involved
200 in matrimony a fortnight, before her father, a hale
and hearty man, died—on purpose, I believe, for the
pleasure of plaguing me with the care of his daughter.
But here comes my helpmate! She appears in great
good humor. How happy I should be if I could tease
her into loving me, though but a little!

Enter LADY TEAZLE.

LADY TEAZ. Lud! Sir Peter, I hope you haven't been
quarreling with Maria—it isn't using me well to be
ill humored when I am not by.

SIR PET. Ah, Lady Teazle, you might have the power
210 to make me good humored at all times.

LADY TEAZ. I am sure I wish I had—for I want you
to be in charming sweet temper at this moment. Do
be good humored now, and let me have two hundred
pounds, will you?

SIR PET. Two hundred pounds! what, an't I to be
in a good humor without paying for it! But speak to
me thus, and i'faith there's nothing I could refuse you.
You shall have it; but seal me a bond for the repay-
ment.

LADY TEAZ. O, no—there—my note of hand will do 220 as well.

SIR PET. (*Kissing her hand.*) And you shall no longer reproach me with not giving you an independent settlement,—I mean shortly to surprise you; but shall we always live thus, hey?

LADY TEAZ. If you please. I'm sure I don't care how soon we leave off quarrelling, provided you'll own *you* were tired first.

SIR PET. Well—then let our future contest be, who shall be most obliging.   230

LADY TEAZ. I assure you, Sir Peter, good nature becomes you. You look now as you did before we were married!—when you used to walk with me under the elms, and tell me stories of what a gallant you were in your youth, and chuck me under the chin, you would, and ask me if I thought I could love an old fellow, who would deny me nothing—didn't you?

SIR PET. Yes, yes, and you were as kind and attentive.

LADY TEAZ. Aye, so I was, and would always take 240 your part, when my acquaintance used to abuse you, and turn you into ridicule.

SIR PET. Indeed!

LADY TEAZ. Aye, and when my cousin Sophy has called you a stiff, peevish old bachelor, and laughed at me for thinking of marrying one who might be my father, I have always defended you—and said, I didn't think you so ugly by any means, and that I dared say you'd make a very good sort of a husband.

SIR PET. And you prophesied right—and we shall 250 certainly now be the happiest couple——

LADY TEAZ. And never differ again!

SIR PET. No, never!—though at the same time, indeed, my dear Lady Teazle, you must watch your temper very narrowly; for in all our little quarrels, my dear, if you recollect, my love, you always began first.

LADY TEAZ. I beg your pardon, my dear Sir Peter: indeed, you always gave the provocation.

SIR PET. Now, see, my angel! take care—*contra-*
260 *dicting* isn't the way to keep friends.

LADY TEAZ. Then, don't *you* begin it, my love!

SIR PET. There, now! you—you are going on—you don't perceive, my life, that you are just doing the very thing which you know always makes me angry.

LADY TEAZ. Nay, you know if you will be angry without any reason——

SIR PET. There now! you want to quarrel again.

LADY TEAZ. No, I am sure I don't—but, if you will be so peevish——

270 SIR PET. There now! who begins first?

LADY TEAZ. Why, you, to be sure. I said nothing—but there's no bearing your temper.

SIR PET. No, no, madam, the fault's in your own temper.

LADY TEAZ. Aye, you are just what my cousin Sophy said you would be.

SIR PET. Your cousin Sophy is a forward, imperti-nent gipsy.

LADY TEAZ. You are a great bear, I'm sure, to abuse
280 my relations.

SIR PET. Now may all the plagues of marriage be doubled on me, if ever I try to be friends with you any more!

LADY TEAZ. So much the better.

SIR PET. No, no, madam; 'tis evident you never cared a pin for me, and I was a madman to marry you—a pert, rural cöquette, that had refused half the honest squires in the neighborhood!

LADY TEAZ. And I am sure I was a fool to marry
290 you—an old dangling bachelor, who was single at fifty, only because he never could meet with any one who would have him.

SIR PET. Aye, aye, madam; but you were pleased

enough to listen to me—*you* never had such an offer before.

LADY TEAZ. No! didn't I refuse Sir Twivy Tarrier, who everybody said would have been a better match —for his estate is just as good as yours—and he has broke his neck since we have been married.

SIR PET. I have done with you, madam! You are 300 an unfeeling, ungrateful—but there's an end of everything. I believe you capable of anything that's bad. Yes, madam, I now believe the reports relative to you and Charles, madam—yes, madam, you and Charles— are not without grounds——

LADY TEAZ. Take care, Sir Peter! you had better not insinuate any such thing! I'll not be suspected with*out cause*, I promise you.

SIR PET. Very well, madam! very well! a separate maintenance as soon as you please. Yes, madam, or a 310 divorce! I'll make an example of myself for the benefit of all old bachelors. Let us separate, madam.

LADY TEAZ. Agreed! agreed! And now, my dear Sir Peter, we are of a mind once more, we may be the *happiest couple,* and *never differ again,* you know: ha! ha! Well, you are going to be in a passion, I see, and I shall only interrupt you—so, bye! bye!   *Exit.*

SIR PET. Plagues and tortures! can't I make her angry neither? Oh, I am the miserablest fellow! But I'll not bear her presuming to keep her temper—no! she 320 may break my heart, but she shan't keep her temper.
                                                    Exit.

SCENE II

CHARLES's *house.*

Enter TRIP, MOSES, *and* SIR OLIVER SURFACE.

TRIP. Here, Master Moses! if you'll stay a moment, I'll try whether—what's the gentleman's name?

SIR OLIV. Mr. Moses, what *is* my name? (*Aside.*)

Mos. Mr. Premium.

TRIP. Premium—very well. *Exit* TRIP, *taking snuff.*

SIR OLIV. To judge by the servants one wouldn't believe the master was ruined. But what!—sure, this was my brother's house?

Mos. Yes, sir; Mr. Charles bought it of Mr. Joseph, 10 with the furniture, pictures, &c., just as the old gentleman left it—Sir Peter thought it a great piece of extravagance in him.

SIR OLIV. In my mind, the other's economy in *selling* it to him was more reprehensible by half.

Re-enter TRIP.

TRIP. My master says you must wait, gentlemen; he has company, and can't speak with you yet.

SIR OLIV. If he knew *who* it was wanted to see him, perhaps he wouldn't have sent such a message?

TRIP. Yes, yes, sir; he knows *you* are here—I didn't 20 forget little Premium—no, no, no.

SIR OLIV. Very well—and I pray, sir, what may be your name?

TRIP. Trip, sir—my name is Trip, at your service.

SIR OLIV. Well, then, Mr. Trip, you have a pleasant sort of a place here, I guess.

TRIP. Why, yes—here are three or four of us pass our time agreeably enough; but then our wages are sometimes a little in arrear—and not very great either —but fifty pounds a year, and find our own bags and 30 bouquets.[5]

SIR OLIV. [*Aside.*] Bags and bouquets! halters and bastinadoes!

TRIP. But *à propos,* Moses, have you been able to get me that little bill discounted?

SIR OLIV. [*Aside.*] Wants to raise money, too!—mercy on me! Has his distresses, I warrant, like a lord, —and affects creditors and duns.

[5] **bags and bouquets** referring to the dress of footmen

Mos. 'Twas not to be done, indeed, Mr. Trip.

(*Gives the note.*)

Trip. Good lack, you surprise me! My friend *Brush* has indorsed it, and I thought when he put his mark 40 on the back of a bill 'twas as good as cash.

Mos. No, 'twouldn't do.

Trip. A small sum—but twenty pounds. Hark'ee, Moses, do you think you couldn't get it me by way of annuity?

Sir Oliv. [*Aside.*] An annuity! ha! ha! ha! a footman raise money by way of annuity! Well done, luxury, egad!

Mos. But you must insure your place.

Trip. Oh, with all my heart! I'll insure my place, 50 and my life too, if you please.

Sir Oliv. [*Aside.*] It's more than I would your neck.

Trip. But then, Moses, it must be done before this d—d register[6] takes place—one wouldn't like to have one's name made public, you know.

Mos. No, certainly. But is there nothing you could deposit?

Trip. Why, nothing capital of my master's wardrobe has dropped lately; but I could give you a mortgage on some of his winter clothes, with equity of re- 60 demption before November—or you shall have the reversion of the French velvet, or a post-obit[7] on the blue and silver;—these, I should think, Moses, with a few pair of point ruffles, as a collateral security— hey, my little fellow?

Mos. Well, well.   (*Bell rings.*)

Trip. Gad, I heard the bell! I believe, gentlemen, I can now introduce you. Don't forget the annuity, little Moses! This way, gentlemen, insure my place, you know.   70

---

[6] **d—d register** referring to the provision in the Annuity Bill for registering life annuities   [7] **post-obit** claim to be satisfied after the death of the original owner

Sɪʀ Oʟɪᴠ. [*Aside.*] If the man be a shadow of his master, this is the temple of dissipation indeed!

Exeunt.

Sᴄᴇɴᴇ III

Cʜᴀʀʟᴇs [Sᴜʀꜰᴀᴄᴇ], Cᴀʀᴇʟᴇss, &c., &c.
at a table with wine, &c.

Cʜᴀs. Sᴜʀꜰ. 'Fore heaven, 'tis true!—there's the great degeneracy of the age. Many of our acquaintance have taste, spirit, and politeness; but, plague on't, they won't drink.

Cᴀʀᴇ. It is so, indeed, Charles! they give in to all the substantial luxuries of the table, and abstain from nothing but wine and wit.

Cʜᴀs. Sᴜʀꜰ. Oh, certainly society suffers by it intolerably! for now, instead of the social spirit of raillery
10 that used to mantle over a glass of bright Burgundy, their conversation is become just like the Spa-water they drink, which has all the pertness and flatulence of champagne, without its spirit or flavor.

1 Gᴇɴᴛ. But what are *they* to do who love play better than wine?

Cᴀʀᴇ. True! there's Harry diets himself for gaming, and is now under a hazard regimen.

Cʜᴀs. Sᴜʀꜰ. Then he'll have the worst of it. What! you wouldn't train a horse for the course by keeping
20 him from corn! For my part, egad, I am now never so successful as when I am a little merry—let me throw on a bottle of champagne, and I never lose—at least I never feel my losses, which is exactly the same thing.

2 Gᴇɴᴛ. Aye, that I believe.

Cʜᴀs. Sᴜʀꜰ. And, then, what man can pretend to be a believer in love, who is an abjurer of wine? 'Tis the test by which the lover knows his own heart. Fill a dozen bumpers to a dozen beauties, and she that floats at top is the maid that has bewitched you.

CARE. Now then, Charles, be honest, and give us 30
your real favorite.

CHAS. SURF. Why, I have withheld her only in com-
passion to you. If I toast her, you must give a round
of her peers—which is impossible—on earth.

CARE. Oh, then we'll find some canonised vestals or
heathen goddesses that will do, I warrant!

CHAS. SURF. Here then, bumpers, you rogues! bumpers! Maria! Maria—   (*Drink.*)

1 GENT. Maria who?

CHAS. SURF. O, damn the surname!—'tis too formal 40
to be registered in Love's calendar—but now, Sir Toby
Bumper, beware—we must have beauty superlativo.

CARE. Nay, never study, Sir Toby: we'll stand to the
toast, though your mistress should want an eye—
and you know you have a song will excuse you.

SIR TOBY. Egad, so I have! and I'll give him the song
instead of the lady.   [*Sings.*]

SONG AND CHORUS

    Here's to the maiden of bashful fifteen;
      Here's to the widow of fifty;
    Here's to the flaunting extravagant quean,   50
      And here's to the housewife that's thrifty.
Chorus.   Let the toast pass—
      Drink to the lass—
I'll warrant she'll prove an excuse for the glass.

    Here's to the charmer whose dimples we prize;
      Now to the maid who has none, sir;
    Here's to the girl with a pair of blue eyes,
      And here's to the nymph with but one, sir.
Chorus.   Let the toast pass, &c.

    Here's to the maid with a bosom of snow: 60
      Now to *her* that's as brown as a berry:
    Here's to the wife with a face full of woe,
      And now for the damsel that's merry.
Chorus.   Let the toast pass, &c.

    For let 'em be clumsy, or let 'em be slim,
      Young or ancient, I care not a feather:

So fill a pint bumper quite up to the brim,
    —And let us e'en toast 'em together.
Chorus.   Let the toast pass, &c.

70   ALL. Bravo! Bravo!

Enter TRIP, *and whispers* CHARLES SURFACE.

CHAS. SURF. Gentlemen, you must excuse me a little.
—Careless, take the chair, will you?

CARE. Nay, prithee, Charles, what now? This is one
of your peerless beauties, I suppose, has dropped in
by chance?

CHAS. SURF. No, faith! To tell you the truth, 'tis a
Jew and a broker, who are come by appointment.

CARE. Oh, damn it! let's have the Jew in—

1 GENT. Aye, and the broker too, by all means.

80   2 GENT. Yes, yes, the Jew and the broker.

CHAS. SURF. Egad, with all my heart!—Trip bid the
gentlemen walk in.—   [*Exit* TRIP.]
Though there's one of them a stranger, I can tell you.

CARE. Charles, let us give them some generous
Burgundy, and perhaps they'll grow conscientious.

CHAS. SURF. Oh, hang 'em, no! wine does but draw
forth a man's *natural* qualities; and to make *them*
drink would only be to whet their knavery.

Enter TRIP, SIR OLIVER SURFACE, *and* MOSES.

CHAS. SURF. So, honest Moses; walk in, pray, Mr.
90 Premium—that's the gentleman's name, isn't it, Moses?

MOS. Yes, sir.

CHAS. SURF. Set chairs, Trip.—Sit down, Mr. Premium.—Glasses, Trip.—Sit down, Moses.— Come, Mr.
Premium, I'll give you a sentiment; here's 'Success to
usury!'—Moses, fill the gentleman a bumper.

MOS. Success to usury!

CARE. Right, Moses—usury is prudence and industry, and deserves to succeed.

SIR OLIV. Then here's— All the success it deserves!

CARE. No, no, that won't do! Mr. Premium, you have 100
demurred to the toast, and must drink it in a pint
bumper.

1 GENT. A pint bumper, at least.

Mos. Oh, pray, sir, consider—Mr. Premium's a
gentleman.

CARE. And therefore loves good wine.

2 GENT. Give Moses a quart glass—this is mutiny,
and a high contempt of the chair.

CARE. Here, now for't! I'll see justice done, to the
last drop of my bottle. 110

SIR OLIV. Nay, pray, gentlemen—I did not expect
this usage.

CHAS. SURF. No, hang it, Careless, you shan't; Mr.
Premium's a stranger.

SIR OLIV. [Aside.] Odd! I wish I was well out of this
company.

CARE. Plague on 'em then! if they won't drink, we'll
not sit down with 'em. Come, Harry, the dice are in
the next room.—Charles, you'll join us—when you
have finished your business with these gentlemen? 120

CHAS. SURF. I will! I will!—Exeunt [Gentlemen].
Careless!

CARE. Well!

CHAS. SURF. Perhaps I may want you.

CARE. Oh, you know I am always ready—word,
note, or bond, 'tis all the same to me. Exit.

Mos. Sir, this is Mr. Premium, a gentleman of the
strictest honor and secrecy; and always performs what
he undertakes. Mr. Premium, this is——

CHAS. SURF. Pshaw! have done! Sir, my friend Moses 130
is a very honest fellow, but a little slow at expression;
he'll be an hour giving us our titles. Mr. Premium, the
plain state of the matter is this—I am an extravagant
young fellow who want[s] money to borrow; you I
take to be a prudent old fellow, who ha[s] got money
to lend. I am blockhead enough to give fifty per cent

sooner than not have it; and you, I presume, are rogue enough to take a hundred if you could get it. Now, sir, you see we are acquainted at once, and may
140 proceed to business without farther ceremony.

Sir Oliv. Exceeding frank, upon my word. I see, sir, you are not a man of many compliments.

Chas. Surf. Oh, no, sir! plain dealing in business I always think best.

Sir Oliv. Sir, I like you the better for't. However, you are mistaken in one thing—I have no money to lend, but I believe I could procure some of a friend; but then he's an unconscionable dog—isn't he, Moses? And must sell stock to accommodate you—mustn't he,
150 Moses?

Mos. Yes, indeed! You know I always speak the truth, and scorn to tell a lie!

Chas. Surf. Right! People that expect truth generally do. But these are trifles, Mr. Premium. What! I know money isn't to be bought without paying for't!

Sir Oliv. Well, but what security could you give? You have no land, I suppose?

Chas. Surf. Not a mole-hill, nor a twig, but what's in beau-pots[8] out at the window!
160 Sir Oliv. Nor any stock, I presume?

Chas. Surf. Nothing but live stock—and that's only a few pointers and ponies. But pray, Mr. Premium, are you acquainted at all with any of my connections?

Sir Oliv. Why, to say truth, I am.

Chas. Surf. Then you must know that I have a devilish rich uncle in the East Indies, Sir *Oliver Surface*, from whom I have the greatest expectations.

Sir Oliv. That you have a wealthy uncle, I have heard—but how your expectations will turn out is
170 more, I believe, than you can tell.

Chas. Surf. Oh, no!—there can be no doubt—they tell me I'm a prodigious favorite—and that he talks of leaving me everything.

[8] **beau-pots** ornamental vases for flowers

Sɪʀ Oʟɪᴠ. Indeed! this is the first I've heard on't.

Cʜᴀs. Sᴜʀꜰ. Yes, yes, 'tis just so.—Moses knows 'tis true; don't you, Moses?

Mos. Oh, yes! I'll swear to't.

Sɪʀ Oʟɪᴠ. [*Aside.*] Egad, they'll persuade me presently I'm at Bengal.

Cʜᴀs. Sᴜʀꜰ. Now I propose, Mr. Premium, if it's 180 agreeable to you, a post-obit on Sir Oliver's life; though at the same time the old fellow has been so liberal to me that I give you my word I should be very sorry to hear anything had happened to him.

Sɪʀ Oʟɪᴠ. Not more than *I* should, I assure you. But the bond you mention happens to be just the worst security you could offer me—for I might live to a hundred and never recover the principal.

Cʜᴀs. Sᴜʀꜰ. Oh, yes, you would!—the moment Sir Oliver dies, you know, you'd come on me for the 190 money.

Sɪʀ Oʟɪᴠ. Then I believe I should be the most unwelcome dun you ever had in your life.

Cʜᴀs. Sᴜʀꜰ. What! I suppose you are afraid now that Sir Oliver is too good a life?

Sɪʀ Oʟɪᴠ. No, indeed I am not—though I have heard he is as hale and healthy as any man of his years in Christendom.

Cʜᴀs. Sᴜʀꜰ. There again you are misinformed. No, no, the climate has hurt him considerably, poor uncle 200 Oliver. Yes, he breaks apace, I'm told—and so much altered lately that his nearest relations don't know him.

Sɪʀ Oʟɪᴠ. No! Ha! ha! ha! so much altered lately that his relations don't know him! Ha! ha! ha! that's droll, egad—ha! ha! ha!

Cʜᴀs. Sᴜʀꜰ. Ha! ha!—you're glad to hear that, little Premium.

Sɪʀ Oʟɪᴠ. No, no, I'm not.

Cʜᴀs. Sᴜʀꜰ. Yes, yes, you are—ha! ha! ha!—you know that mends your chance.   210

Sɪʀ Oʟɪᴠ. But I'm told Sir Oliver is coming over— nay, some say he is actually arrived.

Cʜᴀs. Sᴜʀғ. Pshaw! sure I must know better than you whether he's come or not. No, no, rely on't, he is at this moment at Calcutta, isn't he, Moses?

Mos. Oh, yes, certainly.

Sɪʀ Oʟɪᴠ. Very true, as you say, you must know better than I, though I have it from pretty good authority —haven't I, Moses?

220   Mos. Yes, most undoubted!

Sɪʀ Oʟɪᴠ. But, sir, as I understand you want a few hundreds immediately, is there nothing you would dispose of?

Cʜᴀs. Sᴜʀғ. How do you mean?

Sɪʀ Oʟɪᴠ. For instance, now—I have heard—that your father left behind him a great quantity of massy old plate.

Cʜᴀs. Sᴜʀғ. O lud! that's gone long ago—Moses can tell you how better than I can.

230   Sɪʀ Oʟɪᴠ. Good lack! all the family race-cups and corporation-bowls! (Aside.)—Then it was also supposed that his library was one of the most valuable and complete.

Cʜᴀs. Sᴜʀғ. Yes, yes, so it was—vastly too much so for a private gentleman—for my part, I was always of a communicative disposition, so I thought it a shame to keep so much knowledge to myself.

Sɪʀ Oʟɪᴠ. [Aside.] Mercy on me! learning that had run in the family like an heirloom!—[Aloud.] Pray, 240   what are become of the books?

Cʜᴀs. Sᴜʀғ. You must inquire of the auctioneer, Master Premium, for I don't believe even Moses can direct you there.

Mos. I never meddle with books.

Sɪʀ Oʟɪᴠ. So, so, nothing of the family property left, I suppose?

Cʜᴀs. Sᴜʀғ. Not much, indeed; unless you have a mind to the family pictures. I have got a room full of

ancestors above—and if you have a taste for old paint-
ings, egad, you shall have 'em a bargain!   250

SIR OLIV. Hey! and the devil! sure, you wouldn't
sell your forefathers, would you?

CHAS. SURF. Every man of 'em, to the best bidder.

SIR OLIV. What! your great-uncles and aunts?

CHAS. SURF. Aye, and my great-grandfathers and
grandmothers too.

SIR OLIV. Now I give him up!—(*Aside.*)—What
the plague, have you no bowels for your own kindred?
Odd's life! do you take me for Shylock in the play,
that you would raise money of me on your own flesh 260
and blood?

CHAS. SURF. Nay, my little broker, don't be angry:
what need *you* care, if you have your money's worth?

SIR OLIV. Well, I'll be the purchaser—I think I can
dispose of the family.—[*Aside.*] Oh, I'll never forgive
him this! never!

Enter CARELESS.

CARE. Come, Charles, what keeps you?

CHAS. SURF. I can't come yet. I'faith! we are going
to have a sale above—here's little Premium will buy
all my ancestors!   270

CARE. Oh, burn your ancestors!

CHAS. SURF. No, he may do that afterwards, if he
pleases. Stay, Careless, we want you; egad, you shall
be auctioneer—so come along with us.

CARE. Oh, have with you, if that's the case.—I can
handle a hammer as well as a dice box!

SIR OLIV. [*Aside.*] Oh, the profligates!

CHAS. SURF. Come, Moses, you shall be appraiser,
if we want one.—Gad's life, little Premium, you don't
seem to like the business.   280

SIR OLIV. Oh, yes, I do, vastly! Ha! ha! yes, yes, I
think it a rare joke to sell one's family by auction—
ha! ha!—[*Aside.*] Oh, the prodigal!

CHAS. SURF. To be sure! when a man wants money, where the plague should he get assistance, if he can't make free with his own relations?   *Exeunt.*

End of the third Act.

Act IV

SCENE I

Picture-room at CHARLES'S.

Enter CHARLES SURFACE, SIR OLIVER SURFACE, MOSES, *and* CARELESS.

CHAS. SURF. Walk in, gentlemen, pray walk in!— here they are, the family of the Surfaces, up to the Conquest.

SIR OLIV. And, in my opinion, a goodly collection.

CHAS. SURF. Aye, aye, these are done in true spirit of portrait-painting—no volunteer grace or expression —not like the works of your modern Raphael, who gives you the strongest resemblance, yet contrives to make your own portrait independent of you; so that
10 you may sink the original and not hurt the picture. No, no; the merit of these is the inveterate likeness— all stiff and awkward as the originals, and like nothing in human nature beside!

SIR OLIV. Ah! we shall never see such figures of men again.

CHAS. SURF. I hope not. Well, you see, Master Premium, what a domestic character I am—here I sit of an evening surrounded by my family. But come, get to your pulpit, Mr. Auctioneer—here's an old gouty chair
20 of my grandfather's will answer the purpose.

CARE. Aye, aye, this will do. But, Charles, I have ne'er a hammer; and what's an auctioneer without his hammer?

CHAS. SURF. Egad, that's true. What parchment have we here? (*Takes down a roll.*) 'Richard, heir to Thomas'—our genealogy in full. Here, Careless, you shall have no common bit of mahogany—here's the family tree for you, you rogue—this shall be your hammer, and now you may knock down my ancestors with their own pedigree.   30

SIR OLIV. [*Aside.*] What an unnatural rogue!—an *ex post facto* parricide!

CARE. Yes, yes, here's a list of your generation indeed;—faith, Charles, this is the most convenient thing you could have found for the business, for 'twill serve not only as a hammer, but a catalogue into the bargain.—But come, begin—A-going, a-going, a-going!

CHAS. SURF. Bravo, Careless! Well, here's my great uncle, Sir Richard Raviline, a marvellous good general in his day, I assure you. He served in all the Duke of   40 Marlborough's wars, and got that cut over his eye at the battle of Malplaquet.[1] What say you, Mr. Premium? look at him—there's a hero for you! not cut out of his feathers, as your modern clipped captains are, but enveloped in wig and regimentals, as a general should be. What do you bid?

MOS. Mr. Premium would have you speak.

CHAS. SURF. Why, then, he shall have him for ten pounds, and I am sure that's not dear for a staff-officer.   50

SIR OLIV. [*Aside.*] Heaven deliver me! his famous uncle Richard for ten pounds!—Very well, sir, I take him at that.

CHAS. SURF. Careless, knock down my uncle Richard.—Here, now, is a maiden sister of his, my great-

[1] **battle of Malplaquet** victory over the French, September 11, 1709

aunt Deborah, done by Kneller,[2] thought to be in his best manner, and a very formidable likeness. There she is, you see, a shepherdess feeding her flock. You shall have her for five pounds ten—the sheep are
60 worth the money.

SIR OLIV. [*Aside.*] Ah! poor Deborah! a woman who set such a value on herself!—Five pound ten—she's mine.

CHAS. SURF. Knock down my aunt Deborah! Here, now, are two that were a sort of cousins of theirs.— You see, Moses, these pictures were done some time ago, when beaux wore wigs, and the ladies wore their own hair.

SIR OLIV. Yes, truly, head-dresses appear to have been a little lower in those days.
70 CHAS. SURF. Well, take that couple for the same.

MOS. 'Tis [a] good bargain.

CHAS. SURF. Careless!—This, now, is a grandfather of my mother's, a learned judge, well known on the western circuit.—What do you rate him at, Moses?

MOS. Four guineas.

CHAS. SURF. Four guineas! Gad's life, you don't bid me the price of his wig.—Mr. Premium, *you* have more respect for the woolsack;[3] do let us knock his lordship down at fifteen.
80 SIR OLIV. By all means.

CARE. Gone!

CHAS. SURF. And there are two brothers of his, William and Walter Blunt, Esquires, both members of Parliament, and noted speakers; and, what's very extraordinary, I believe this is the first time they were ever bought and sold.

SIR OLIV. That's very extraordinary, indeed! I'll take them at your own price, for the honor of Parliament.

---

[2] **Kneller** Sir Godfrey Kneller (1646-1723), a famous portrait painter   [3] **respect for the woolsack** respect for judges (who sat on seats made of bags of wool when they attended the House of Lords)

CARE. Well said, little Premium! I'll knock 'em
down at forty.   90

CHAS. SURF. Here's a jolly fellow—I don't know
what relation, but he was mayor of Manchester; take
him at eight pounds.

SIR OLIV. No, no—six will do for the mayor.

CHAS. SURF. Come, make it guineas, and I'll throw
you the two aldermen there into the bargain.

SIR OLIV. They're mine.

CHAS. SURF. Careless, knock down the mayor and
aldermen. But, plague on't! we shall be all day retail-
ing in this manner; do let us deal wholesale—what   100
say you, little Premium? Give me three hundred
pounds for the rest of the family in the lump.

CARE. Aye, aye, that will be the best way.

SIR OLIV. Well, well, anything to accommodate you;
they are mine. But there is one portrait which you
have always passed over.

CARE. What, that ill-looking little fellow over the
settee?

SIR OLIV. Yes, sir, I mean that; though I don't think
him so ill-looking a little fellow, by any means.   110

CHAS. SURF. What, that? Oh, that's my uncle Oliver!
'Twas done before he went to India.

CARE. Your uncle Oliver! Gad, then you'll never be
friends, Charles. That, now, to me, is as stern a looking rogue as ever I saw—an unforgiving eye, and a
damned disinheriting countenance! an inveterate
knave, depend on't. Don't you think so, little Premium?

SIR OLIV. Upon my soul, sir, I do not; I think it is
as honest a looking face as any in the room, dead or
alive. But I suppose your uncle Oliver goes with the   120
rest of the lumber?

CHAS. SURF. No, hang it! I'll not part with poor
Noll. The old fellow has been very good to me, and,
egad, I'll keep his picture while I've a room to put it
in.

SIR OLIV. The rogue's my nephew after all! (*Aside.*)
—But, sir, I have somehow taken a fancy to that picture.

CHAS. SURF. I'm sorry for't, for you certainly will
130 not have it. Oons! haven't you got enough of 'em?

SIR OLIV. I forgive him everything! (*Aside.*)—But,
sir, when I take a whim in my head, I don't value
money. I'll give you as much for that as for all the rest.

CHAS. SURF. Don't tease me, master broker; I tell
you I'll not part with it, and there's an end on't.

SIR OLIV. How like his father the dog is!—(*Aloud.*)
Well, well, I have done.—I did not perceive it before,
but I think I never saw such a resemblance.—Well,
sir—here is a draught for your sum.

140 CHAS SURF. Why, 'tis for eight hundred pounds!

SIR OLIV. You will not let Sir Oliver go?

CHAS. SURF. Zounds! no! I tell you, once more.

SIR OLIV. Then never mind the difference; we'll
balance another time. But give me your hand on the
bargain; you are an honest fellow, Charles—I beg
pardon, sir, for being so free.—Come, Moses.

CHAS. SURF. Egad, this is a whimsical old fellow!—
but hark'ee, Premium, you'll prepare lodgings for
these gentlemen.

150 SIR OLIV. Yes, yes, I'll send for them in a day or
two.

CHAS. SURF. But hold—do now—send a genteel
conveyance for them, for, I assure you, they were most
of them used to ride in their own carriages.

SIR OLIV. I will, I will, for all but—Oliver.

CHAS. SURF. Aye, all but the little honest nabob.

SIR OLIV. You're fixed on that?

CHAS. SURF. Peremptorily.

SIR OLIV. A dear extravagant rogue!—Good day!—
160 Come, Moses,—Let me hear now who dares call him
profligate!   *Exeunt* SIR OLIVER *and* MOSES.

CARE. Why, this is the oddest genius of the sort I
ever saw!

CHAS. SURF. Egad, he's the prince of brokers, I think. I wonder how the devil Moses got acquainted with so honest a fellow.—Ha! here's Rowley.—Do, Careless, say I'll join the company in a moment.

CARE. I will—but don't let that old blockhead persuade you to squander any of that money on old musty debts, or any such nonsense; for tradesmen, Charles, 170 are the most exorbitant fellows!

CHAS. SURF. Very true, and paying them is only encouraging them.

CARE. Nothing else.

CHAS. SURF. Aye, aye, never fear.—*Exit* CARELESS. So! this was an odd old fellow, indeed! Let me see, two-thirds of this is mine by right—five hundred and thirty pounds. 'Fore heaven! I find one's ancestors are more valuable relations than I took 'em for!—Ladies and gentlemen, your most obedient and very grateful 180 humble servant.

Enter ROWLEY.

Ha! old Rowley! egad, you are just come in time to take leave of your old acquaintance.

ROW. Yes, I heard they were going. But I wonder you can have such spirits under so many distresses.

CHAS. SURF. Why, there's the point—my distresses are so many, that I can't afford to part with my spirits; but I shall be rich and splenetic, all in good time. However, I suppose you are surprised that I am not more sorrowful at parting with so many near relations; 190 to be sure, 'tis very affecting; but, rot 'em, you see they never move a muscle, so why should I?

ROW. There's no making you serious a moment.

CHAS. SURF. Yes, faith: I am so now. Here, my honest Rowley, here, get me this changed, and take a hundred pounds of it immediately to old Stanley.

ROW. A hundred pounds! Consider only——

CHAS. SURF. Gad's life, don't talk about it! poor Stanley's wants are pressing, and, if you don't make

200 haste, we shall have some one call that has a better right to the money.

Row. Ah! there's the point! I never will cease dunning you with the old proverb——

Chas. Surf. 'Be *just* before you're *generous,*' hey! —Why, so I would if I could; but Justice is an old lame hobbling beldame, and I can't get her to keep pace with Generosity, for the soul of me.

Row. Yet, Charles, believe me, one hour's reflection——

210 Chas. Surf. Aye, aye, it's all very true; but, hark'ee, Rowley, while I have, by heaven I'll give—so, damn your economy! and now for hazard.   *Exit.*

Scene II

The parlor.

Enter Sir Oliver Surface *and* Moses.

Mos. Well, sir, I think, as Sir Peter said, you have seen Mr. Charles in high glory; 'tis great pity he's so extravagant.

Sir Oliv. True, but he wouldn't sell my picture.

Mos. And loves wine and women so much.

Sir Oliv. But he wouldn't sell my picture!

Mos. And game[s] so deep.

Sir Oliv. But he wouldn't sell my picture. Oh, here's Rowley.

Enter Rowley.

10 Row. So, Sir Oliver, I find you have made a purchase——

Sir Oliv. Yes, yes, our young rake has parted with his ancestors like old tapestry.

Row. And here has he commissioned me to redeliver you part of the purchase-money—I mean, though, in your necessitous character of old *Stanley.*

Mos. Ah! there is the pity of all: he is so damned charitable.

Row. And I left a hosier and two tailors in the hall, who, I'm sure, won't be paid, and this hundred would 20 satisfy 'em.

Sir Oliv. Well, well, I'll pay his debts—and his benevolence too; but now I am no more a broker, and you shall introduce me to the elder brother as old Stanley.

Row. Not yet awhile; Sir Peter, I know, means to call there about this time.

Enter Trip

Trip. O gentlemen, I beg pardon for not showing you out; this way—Moses, a word.

Exeunt Trip *and* Moses.

Sir Oliv. There's a fellow for you! Would you be- 30 lieve it, that puppy intercepted the Jew on our coming, and wanted to raise money before he got to his master!

Row. Indeed!

Sir Oliv. Yes, they are now planning an annuity business. Ah, Master Rowley, in my days, servants were content with the follies of their masters, when they were worn a little threadbare—but now they have their vices, like their birthday clothes,[4] with the gloss on.   *Exeunt.* 40

Scene III

A library [*in* Joseph Surface's *house.*]

Joseph Surface *and Servant.*

Jos. Surf. No letter from Lady Teazle?

Serv. No, sir.

Jos. Surf. [*Aside.*] I am surprised she hasn't sent, if

[4] **birthday clothes** worn on the king's birthday

she is prevented from coming. Sir Peter certainly does not suspect me. Yet I wish I may not lose the heiress, through the scrape I have drawn myself in with the wife; however, Charles's imprudence and bad character are great points in my favor.   (*Knocking.*)

SERV. Sir, I believe that must be Lady Teazle.

10   JOS. SURF. Hold! See whether it is or not, before you go to the door—I have a particular message for you, if it should be my brother.

SERV. 'Tis her ladyship, sir; she always leaves her chair at the milliner's in the next street.

JOS. SURF. Stay, stay—draw that screen before the window—that will do;—my opposite neighbor is a maiden lady of so curious a temper.—(*Servant draws the screen, and exit.*) I have a difficult hand to play in this affair. Lady Teazle has lately suspected my views

20 on Maria; but she must by no means be let into that secret,—at least, not till I have her more in my power.

Enter LADY TEAZLE.

LADY TEAZ. What, sentiment in soliloquy! Have you been very impatient now? O lud! don't pretend to look grave. I vow I couldn't come before.

JOS. SURF. O madam, punctuality is a species of constancy, a very unfashionable quality in a lady.

LADY TEAZ. Upon my word, you ought to pity me. Do you know that Sir Peter is grown so ill-tempered to me of late, and so jealous of *Charles* too—that's the

30 best of the story, isn't it?

JOS. SURF. (*Aside.*) I am glad my scandalous friends keep that up.

LADY TEAZ. I am sure I wish he would let Maria marry him, and then perhaps he would be convinced; don't you, Mr. Surface?

JOS. SURF. (*Aside.*) Indeed I do not.—Oh, certainly I do! for then my dear Lady Teazle would also be convinced how wrong her suspicions were of my having any design on the silly girl.

LADY TEAZ. Well, well, I'm inclined to believe you. 40
But isn't it provoking, to have the most ill-natured
things said to one? And there's my friend Lady Sneerwell has circulated I don't know how many scandalous
tales of me! and all without any foundation, too—
that's what vexes me.

JOS. SURF. Aye, madam, to be sure, that *is* the provoking circumstance—without foundation! yes, yes,
there's the mortification, indeed; for, when a scandalous story is believed against one, there certainly is no
comfort like the consciousness of having deserved it. 50

LADY TEAZ. No, to be sure—then I'd forgive their
malice; but to attack me, who am really so innocent,
and who never say an ill-natured thing of anybody—
that is, of any friend—and then Sir Peter, too, to have
him so peevish, and so suspicious, when I know the
integrity of my own heart—indeed 'tis monstrous!

JOS. SURF. But, my dear Lady Teazle, 'tis your own
fault if you suffer it. When a husband entertains a
groundless suspicion of his wife, and withdraws his
confidence from her, the original compact is broke, 60
and she owes it to the honor of her sex to endeavor to
outwit him.

LADY TEAZ. Indeed! So that, if he suspects me without cause, it follows that the best way of curing his
jealousy is to give him reason for't?

JOS. SURF. Undoubtedly—for your husband should
never be deceived in you: and in that case it becomes
you to be frail in compliment to *his* discernment.

LADY TEAZ. To be sure, what you say is very reason-
able, and when the consciousness of my own inno- 70
cence——

JOS. SURF. Ah, my dear madam, there is the great
mistake; 'tis this very conscious innocence that is of
the greatest prejudice to you. What is it makes you
negligent of forms, and careless of the world's opinion?
why, the *consciousness* of your innocence. What makes
you thoughtless in your conduct, and apt to run into

a thousand little imprudences? why, the *consciousness* of your innocence. What makes you impatient of Sir
80 Peter's temper and outrageous at his suspicions? why, the *consciousness* of your own innocence!

LADY TEAZ. 'Tis very true!

JOS. SURF. Now, my dear Lady Teazle, if you would but once make a trifling *faux pas,* you can't conceive how cautious you would grow—and how ready to humor and agree with your husband.

LADY TEAZ. Do you think so?

JOS. SURF. Oh, I'm sure on't; and then you would find all scandal would cease at once, for—in short,
90 your character at present is like a person in a plethora, absolutely dying of too much health.

LADY TEAZ. So, so; then I perceive your prescription is, that I must sin in my own defence, and part with my virtue to preserve my reputation?

JOS. SURF. Exactly so, upon my credit, ma'am.

LADY TEAZ. Well, certainly this is the oddest doctrine, and the newest receipt for avoiding calumny?

JOS. SURF. An infallible one, believe me. *Prudence,* like *experience,* must be paid for.
100 LADY TEAZ. Why, if my understanding were once convinced——

JOS. SURF. Oh, certainly, madam, your understanding *should* be convinced. Yes, yes—heaven forbid I should persuade you to do anything you *thought* wrong. No, no, I have too much honor to desire it.

LADY TEAZ. Don't you think we may as well leave honor out of the argument?

JOS. SURF. Ah, the ill effects of your country education, I see, still remain with you.
110 LADY TEAZ. I doubt they do, indeed; and I will fairly own to you, that if I could be persuaded to do wrong, it would be by Sir Peter's ill-usage sooner than your honorable logic, after all.

JOS. SURF. Then, by this hand, which he is unworthy of——   [*Taking her hand.*]

Re-enter Servant.

'Sdeath, you blockhead—what do you want?

SERV. I beg pardon, sir, but I thought you wouldn't choose Sir Peter to come up without announcing him.

JOS. SURF. Sir Peter!—Oons—the devil!

LADY TEAZ. Sir Peter! O lud! I'm ruined! I'm ruined! 120

SERV. Sir, 'twasn't I let him in.

LADY TEAZ. Oh! I'm undone! What will become of me, now, Mr. Logic?—Oh! mercy, he's on the stairs— I'll get behind here—and if ever I'm so imprudent again——   (*Goes behind the screen.*)

JOS. SURF. Give me that book.

(*Sits down. Servant pretends to adjust his hair.*)

Enter SIR PETER TEAZLE.

SIR PET. Aye, ever improving himself!—Mr. Surface, Mr. Surface——

JOS. SURF. Oh, my dear Sir Peter, I beg your pardon. (*Gaping, and throws away the book.*) I have been 130 dozing over a stupid book. Well, I am much obliged to you for this call. You haven't been here, I believe, since I fitted up this room. Books, you know, are the only things I am a coxcomb in.

SIR PET. 'Tis very neat indeed. Well, well, that's proper; and you make even your screen a source of knowledge- -hung, I perceive, with maps.

JOS. SURF. Oh, yes, I find great use in that screen.

SIR PET. I dare say you must—certainly—when you want to find anything in a hurry.   140

JOS. SURF. [*Aside.*] Aye, or to hide anything in a hurry either.

SIR PET. Well, I have a little private business——

JOS. SURF. You needn't stay. (*To Servant.*)

SERV. No, sir.   *Exit.*

JOS. SURF. Here's a chair, Sir Peter—I beg——

SIR PET. Well, now we are alone, there is a subject, my dear friend, on which I wish to unburden my mind

to you—a point of the greatest moment to my peace:
150 in short, my good friend, Lady Teazle's conduct of
late has made me extremely unhappy.

Jos. Surf. Indeed! I am very sorry to hear it.

Sir Pet. Yes, 'tis but too plain she has not the least
regard for me; but, what's worse, I have pretty good
authority to suspect she must have formed an attachment to another.

Jos. Surf. You astonish me!

Sir Pet. Yes! and, between ourselves, I think I have
discovered the person.

160 Jos. Surf. How! you alarm me exceedingly.

Sir Pet. Aye, my dear friend, I knew you would
sympathize with me!

Jos. Surf. Yes, believe me, Sir Peter, such a discovery would hurt me just as much as it would you.

Sir Pet. I am convinced of it.—Ah! it is a happiness
to have a friend whom one can trust even with one's
family secrets. But have you no guess who I mean?

Jos. Surf. I haven't the most distant idea. It can't
be Sir Benjamin Backbite!

170 Sir Pet. O, no! What say you to Charles?

Jos. Surf. My brother! impossible!

Sir Pet. Ah, my dear friend, the goodness of your
own heart misleads you—you judge of others by yourself.

Jos. Surf. Certainly, Sir Peter, the heart that is conscious of its own integrity is ever slow to credit another's treachery.

Sir. Pet. True; but your brother has no sentiment
—you never hear him talk so.

180 Jos. Surf. Yet I can't but think Lady Teazle herself
has too much principle——

Sir Pet. Aye; but what's her principle against the
flattery of a handsome, lively young fellow?

Jos. Surf. That's very true.

Sir Pet. And then, you know, the difference of our
ages makes it very improbable that she should have

any great affection for me; and if she were to be frail, and I were to make it public, why the town would only laugh at me, the foolish old bachelor who had married a girl. 190

Jos. Surf. That's true, to be sure—they *would* laugh.

Sir Pet. Laugh! aye, and make ballads, and paragraphs, and the devil knows what of me.

Jos. Surf. No, you must never make it public.

Sir Pet. But then again—that the nephew of my old friend, Sir Oliver, should be the person to attempt such a wrong, hurts me more nearly.

Jos. Surf. Aye, there's the point. When ingratitude barbs the dart of injury, the wound has double danger in it. 200

Sir Pet. Aye—I, that was, in a manner, left his guardian—in whose house he had been so often entertained—who never in my life denied him—my advice!

Jos. Surf. Oh, 'tis not to be credited! There *may* be a man capable of such baseness, to be sure; but, for my part, till you can give me positive proofs, I cannot but doubt it. However, if it should be proved on him, he is no longer a brother of mine! I disclaim kindred with him—for the man who can break through 210 the laws of hospitality, and attempt the wife of his friend, deserves to be branded as the pest of society.

Sir Pet. What a difference there is between you! What noble sentiments!

Jos. Surf. Yet I cannot suspect Lady Teazle's honor.

Sir Pet. I am sure I wish to think well of her, and to remove all ground of quarrel between us. She has lately reproached me more than once with having made no settlement on her; and, in our last quarrel, she almost hinted that she should not break her heart 220 if I was dead. Now, as we seem to differ in our ideas of expense, I have resolved she shall be her own mistress in that respect for the future; and, if I *were* to die, she shall find that I have not been inattentive to her interest while living. Here, my friend, are the drafts of two deeds, which I wish to have your opinion on. By one, she will enjoy eight hundred a year independent while I live; and, by the other, the bulk of my fortune after my death.

230   Jos. Surf. This conduct, Sir Peter, is indeed truly generous.— (*Aside.*) I wish it may not corrupt my pupil.

Sir Pet. Yes, I am determined she shall have no cause to complain, though I would not have her acquainted with the latter instance of my affection yet awhile.

Jos. Surf. Nor I, if I could help it.   (*Aside.*)

Sir Pet. And now, my dear friend, if you please, we will talk over the situation of your hopes with
240   *Maria.*

Jos. Surf. (*Softly.*) No, no, Sir Peter; another time, if you please.

Sir Pet. I am sensibly chagrined at the little progress you seem to make in her affection.

Jos. Surf. I beg you will not mention it. What are my disappointments when your happiness is in debate! (*Softly.*)—'Sdeath, I shall be ruined every way!
(*Aside.*)

Sir Pet. And though you are so averse to my acquainting Lady Teazle with your passion, I am sure
250   she's not your enemy in the affair.

Jos. Surf. Pray, Sir Peter, now oblige me. I am really too much affected by the subject we have been speaking on to bestow a thought on my own concerns. The man who is entrusted with his friend's distresses can never——

Enter Servant.

Well, sir?

Serv. Your brother, sir, is speaking to a gentleman in the street, and says he knows you are within.

Jos. Surf. 'Sdeath, blockhead—I'm not within—
I'm out for the day.   260

Sir Pet. Stay—hold—a thought has struck me—
you shall be at home.

Jos. Surf. Well, well, let him up.—*Exit Servant.*
He'll interrupt Sir Peter—however—

Sir Pet. Now, my good friend, oblige me, I entreat
you. Before Charles comes, let me conceal myself
somewhere; then do you tax him on the point we have
been talking on, and his answers may satisfy me at
once.

Jos. Surf. O, fie, Sir Peter! would you have me join   270
in so mean a trick?—to trepan my brother too?

Sir Pet. Nay, you tell me you are *sure* he is innocent; if so, you do him the greatest service by giving him an opportunity to clear himself, and you will
set my heart at rest. Come, you shall not refuse me;
here, behind the screen will be (*Goes to the screen.*)
—Hey! what the devil! there seems to be *one* listener
here already—I'll swear I saw a petticoat!

Jos. Surf. Ha! ha! ha! Well, this is ridiculous
enough. I'll tell you, Sir Peter, though I hold a man   280
of intrigue to be a most despicable character, yet you
know, it doesn't follow that one is to be an absolute
Joseph either! Hark'ee! 'tis a little French milliner, a
silly rogue that plagues me—and having some character—on your coming, she ran behind the screen.

Sir Pet. Ah, you rogue!—But, egad, she has overheard all I have been saying of my wife.

Jos. Surf. Oh, 'twill never go any further, you may
depend on't!

Sir Pet. No! then, i'faith, let her hear it out.—   290
Here's a closet will do as well.

Jos. Surf. Well, go in then.

Sir Pet. Sly rogue! sly rogue!

(*Goes into the closet.*)

Jos. Surf. A very narrow escape, indeed! and a curious situation I'm in, to part man and wife in this manner.

LADY TEAZ. (*Peeping from the screen.*) Couldn't I steal off?

JOS. SURF. Keep close, my angel!

300   SIR PET. (*Peeping out.*) Joseph, tax him home.

JOS. SURF. Back, my dear friend!

LADY TEAZ. (*Peeping.*) Couldn't you lock Sir Peter in?

JOS. SURF. Be still, my life!

SIR PET. (*Peeping.*) You're sure the little milliner won't blab?

JOS. SURF. In, in, my dear Sir Peter!—'Fore gad, I wish I had a key to the door.

Enter CHARLES SURFACE.

CHAS. SURF. Hollo! brother, what has been the matter?
310 ter? Your fellow would not let me up at first. What! have you had a Jew or a wench with you?

JOS. SURF. Neither, brother, I assure you.

CHAS. SURF. But what has made Sir Peter steal off? I thought he had been with you.

JOS. SURF. He was, brother; but, hearing *you* were coming, he did not choose to stay.

CHAS. SURF. What! was the old gentleman afraid I wanted to borrow money of him!

JOS. SURF. No, sir, but I am sorry to find, Charles,
320 that you have lately given that worthy man grounds for great uneasiness.

CHAS. SURF. Yes, they tell me I do that to a great many worthy men. But how so, pray?

JOS. SURF. To be plain with you, brother, he thinks you are endeavoring to gain Lady Teazle's affections from him.

CHAS. SURF. Who, I? O lud! not I, upon my word. —Ha! ha! ha! so the old fellow has found out that he has got a young wife, has he?—or, what's worse, has
330 her ladyship discovered that she has an old husband?

Jos. Surf. This is no subject to jest on, brother.—
He who can laugh——

Chas. Surf. True, true, as you were going to say—
then, seriously, I never had the least idea of what you
charge me with, upon my honor.

Jos. Surf. Well, it will give Sir Peter great satisfaction to hear this. (*Aloud*.)

Chas. Surf. To be sure, I once thought the lady
seemed to have taken a fancy to me; but, upon my
soul, I never gave her the least encouragement. Be-   340
sides, you know my attachment to Maria.

Jos. Surf. But sure, brother, even if Lady Teazle
had betrayed the fondest partiality for you——

Chas. Surf. Why, look'ee, Joseph, I hope I shall
never deliberately do a dishonorable action—but if a
pretty woman were purposely to throw herself in my
way—and that pretty woman married to a man old
enough to be her father——

Jos. Surf. Well!

Chas. Surf. Why, I believe I should be obliged to   350
borrow a little of your morality, that's all.—But,
brother, do you know now that you surprise me exceedingly, by naming *me* with Lady Teazle; for, faith,
I alway[s] understood *you* were her favorite.

Jos. Surf. Oh, for shame, Charles! This retort is
foolish.

Chas. Surf. Nay, I swear I have seen you exchange
such significant glances——

Jos. Surf. Nay, nay, sir, this is no jest——

Chas. Surf. Egad, I'm serious! Don't you remember   360
—one day, when I called here——

Jos. Surf. Nay, prithee, Charles——

Chas. Surf. And found you together——

Jos. Surf. Zounds, sir, I insist——

Chas. Surf. And another time, when your servant——

Jos. Surf. Brother, brother, a word with you!—
(*Aside*.) Gad, I must stop him.

CHAS. SURF. Informed me, I say, that——

370   JOS. SURF. Hush! I beg your pardon, but Sir Peter has overheard all we have been saying—I knew you would clear yourself, or I should not have consented.

CHAS. SURF. How, Sir Peter! Where is he?

JOS. SURF. Softly, there! (*Points to the closet.*)

CHAS. SURF. Oh, 'fore heaven, I'll have him out.— Sir Peter, come forth!

JOS. SURF. No, no——

CHAS. SURF. I say, Sir Peter, come into court.— (*Pulls in* SIR PETER.) What! my old guardian!—What

380   —turn inquisitor, and take evidence, incog.?

SIR PET. Give me your hand, Charles—I believe I have suspected you wrongfully—but you mustn't be angry with Joseph—'twas my plan!

CHAS. SURF. Indeed!

SIR PET. But I acquit you. I promise you I don't think near so ill of you as I did. What I have heard has given me great satisfaction.

CHAS. SURF. Egad, then, 'twas lucky you didn't hear any more. Wasn't it, Joseph?   (*Half aside.*)

390   SIR PET. Ah! you would have retorted on him.

CHAS. SURF. Aye, aye, that was a joke.

SIR PET. Yes, yes, I know his honor too well.

CHAS. SURF. But you might as well have suspected him as me in this matter, for all that. Mightn't he, Joseph?   (*Half aside.*)

SIR PET. Well, well, I believe you.

JOS. SURF. [*Aside*]. Would they were both out of the room!

SIR PET. And in future, perhaps, we may not be such strangers.

Enter Servant who whispers JOSEPH SURFACE.

400   JOS. SURF. Lady Sneerwell!—stop her by all means —(*Exit Servant.*) Gentlemen—I beg pardon—I must wait on you downstairs—here's a person come on particular business.

CHAS. SURF. Well, you can see him in another room.

Sir Peter and I haven't met a long time, and I have something to say to him.

Jos. Surf. They must not be left together.—I'll send Lady Sneerwell away, and return directly.— (*Aside.*) Sir Peter, not a word of the French milliner.

Exit Joseph Surface.

Sir Pet. Oh! not for the world!—Ah, Charles, if you 410 associated more with your brother, one might indeed hope for your reformation. He is a man of sentiment. —Well, there is nothing in the world so noble as a man of sentiment!

Chas. Surf. Pshaw! he is too moral by half, and so apprehensive of his good name, as he calls it, that I suppose he would as soon let a priest into his house as a girl.

Sir Pet. No, no,—come, come,—you wrong him. No, no, Joseph is no rake, but he is not such a saint 420 in that respect either,—I have a great mind to tell him—we should have a laugh!   (*Aside.*)

Chas. Surf. Oh, hang him! he's a very anchorite, a young hermit!

Sir Pet. Hark'ee—you must not abuse him; he may chance to hear of it again, I promise you.

Chas. Surf. Why, you won't tell him?

Sir Pet. No—but—this way.—[*Aside.*] Egad, I'll tell him.—Hark'ee, have you a mind to have a good laugh at Joseph?   430

Chas. Surf. I should like it of all things.

Sir Pet. Then, i'faith, we will!—I'll be quit with him for discovering me. (*Aside.*)—He had a girl with him when I called.

Chas. Surf. What! Joseph? you jest.

Sir Pet. Hush!—a little—French milliner—and the best of the jest is—she's in the room now.

Chas. Surf. The devil she is!

Sir Pet. Hush! I tell you. (*Points* [*to the screen*].)

Chas. Surf. Behind the screen! 'Slife, let's unveil 440 her!

SIR PET. No, no, he's coming:—you shan't, indeed!

CHAS. SURF. Oh, egad, we'll have a peep at the little milliner!

SIR PET. Not for the world!—Joseph will never forgive me.

CHAS. SURF. I'll stand by you——

SIR PET. (*Struggling with Charles.*) Odds, here he is!

> JOSEPH SURFACE *enters just as* CHARLES *throws down the screen.*

450   CHAS. SURF. Lady Teazle, by all that's wonderful!

SIR PET. Lady Teazle, by all that's horrible!

CHAS. SURF. Sir Peter, this is one of the smartest French milliners I ever saw. Egad, you seem all to have been diverting yourselves here at hide and seek—and I don't see who is out of the secret. Shall I beg your ladyship to inform me?—Not a word!—Brother, will you please to explain this matter? What! Morality dumb too!—Sir Peter, though I *found* you in the dark, perhaps you are not so now! All mute! Well—though

450   I can make nothing of the affair, I suppose you perfectly understand one another; so I'll leave you to yourselves.—(*Going.*) Brother, I'm sorry to find you *have given that worthy man so much uneasiness,*—Sir Peter! there's nothing *in the world* so *noble as a man of sentiment!*

> *Exit* CHARLES.
> ([*They*] *stand for some time looking at each other.*)

JOS. SURF. Sir Peter—notwithstanding I confess that appearances are against me—if you will afford me your patience—I make no doubt but I shall explain everything to your satisfaction.

470   SIR PET. If you please—

JOS. SURF. The fact is, sir, Lady Teazle, knowing my pretensions to your ward Maria—I say, sir, Lady Teazle, being apprehensive of the jealousy of your temper—and knowing my friendship to the family—

she, sir, I say—called here—in order that—I might explain those pretensions—but on your coming—being apprehensive—as I said—of your jealousy—she withdrew—and this, you may depend on't is the whole truth of the matter.

SIR PET. A very clear account, upon my word; and   480
I dare swear the lady will vouch for every article of it.

LADY TEAZ. (*Coming forward.*) For not one word of it, Sir Peter!

SIR PET. How! don't you think it worth while to agree in the lie?

LADY TEAZ. There is not one syllable of truth in what that gentleman has told you.

SIR PET. I believe you, upon my soul, ma'am!

JOS. SURF. (*Aside.*) 'Sdeath, madam, will you betray   490
me?

LADY TEAZ. Good Mr. Hypocrite, by your leave, I will speak for myself.

SIR PET. Aye, let her alone, sir; you'll find she'll make out a better story than *you,* without prompting.

LADY TEAZ. Hear me, Sir Peter!—I came here on no matter relating to your ward, and even ignorant of this gentleman's pretensions to her—but I came, seduced by his insidious arguments, at least to listen to his pretended passion, if not to sacrifice *your* honor   500
to his baseness.

SIR PET. Now, I believe, the truth *is* coming, indeed!

JOS. SURF. The woman's mad!

LADY TEAZ. No, sir; she has recovered her senses, and your own arts have furnished her with the means.
—Sir Peter, I do not expect you to credit me—but the tenderness you expressed for me, when I am sure you could not think I was a witness to it, has penetrated to my heart, and had I left the place without the shame of this discovery, my future life should have   510
spoke[n] the sincerity of my gratitude. As for that smooth-tongue hypocrite, who would have seduced

the wife of his too credulous friend, while he affected
honorable addresses to his ward—I behold him now
in a light so truly despicable, that I shall never again
respect myself for having listened to him.   *Exit.*

Jos. Surf. Nothwithstanding all this, Sir Peter,
heaven knows——

Sir Pet. That you are a villain!—and so I leave you
520 to your conscience.

Jos. Surf. You are too rash, Sir Peter; you shall
hear me. The man who shuts out conviction by re-
fusing to——

Sir Pet. Oh!—

Exeunt, Joseph Surface *following and speaking.*
End of Act 4th.

Act V

Scene I

The library [in Joseph Surface's *house.]*

Enter Joseph Surface *and Servant.*

Jos. Surf. Mr. Stanley! why should you think I
would see him? you *must* know he comes to ask something.

Serv. Sir, I should not have let him in, but that
Mr. Rowley came to the door with him.

Jos. Surf. Pshaw! blockhead! to suppose that I
should *now* be in a temper to receive visits from poor
relations!—Well, why don't you show the fellow up?

Serv. I will, sir.—Why, sir, it was not my fault that
10 Sir Peter discovered my lady——

Jos. Surf. Go, fool!   *Exit Servant.*

Sure, Fortune never played a man of my policy such a trick before! My character with Sir Peter, my hopes with Maria, destroyed in a moment! I'm in a rare humor to listen to other people's distresses! I shan't be able to bestow even a benevolent sentiment on Stanley.—So! here he comes, and Rowley with him. I must try to recover myself—and put a little charity into my face, however.   *Exit.*

Enter Sir Oliver Surface *and* Rowley.

Sir Oliv. What! does he avoid us? That was he, 20 was it not?

Row. It was, sir—but I doubt you are come a little too abruptly—his nerves are so weak, that the sight of a poor relation may be too much for him.—I should have gone first to break you to him.

Sir Oliv. A plague of his nerves!—Yet this is he whom Sir Peter extols as a man of the most benevolent way of thinking!

Row. As to his way of thinking, I cannot pretend to decide; for, to do him justice, he appears to have 30 as much speculative benevolence as any private gentleman in the kingdom, though he is seldom so sensual as to indulge himself in the exercise of it.

Sir Oliv. Yet has a string of charitable sentiments, I suppose, at his fingers' ends!

Row. Or, rather, at his tongue's end, Sir Oliver; for I believe there is no sentiment he has more faith in than that 'Charity begins at home.'

Sir Oliv. And his, I presume, is of that domestic sort which never stirs abroad at all.   40

Row. I doubt you'll find it so;—but he's coming—I mustn't seem to interrupt you; and you know, immediately as you leave him, I come in to announce your arrival in your real character.

Sir Oliv. True; and afterwards you'll meet me at Sir Peter's.

Row. Without losing a moment.   *Exit* Rowley.

SIR OLIV. So! I don't like the complaisance of his features.

Re-enter JOSEPH SURFACE.

50 JOS. SURF. Sir, I beg you ten thousand pardons for keeping you a moment waiting—Mr. Stanley, I presume.

SIR OLIV. At your service.

JOS. SURF. Sir, I beg you will do me the honor to sit down—I entreat you, sir.

SIR OLIV. Dear sir—there's no occasion.—Too civil by half! (*Aside.*)

JOS. SURF. I have not the pleasure of knowing you, Mr. Stanley; but I am extremely happy to see you 60 look so well. You were nearly related to my mother, I think, Mr. Stanley?

SIR OLIV. I was, sir—so nearly that my present poverty, I fear, may do discredit to her wealthy children —else I should not have presumed to trouble you.

JOS. SURF. Dear sir, there needs no apology: he that is in distress, though a stranger, has a right to claim kindred with the wealthy;—I am sure I wish *I* was one of that class, and had it in my power to offer you even a small relief.

70 SIR OLIV. If your uncle, Sir Oliver, were here, I should have a friend.

JOS. SURF. I wish he were, sir, with all my heart: you should not want an advocate with him, believe me, sir.

SIR OLIV. I should not *need* one—my distresses would recommend me; but I imagined his bounty had enabled *you* to become the agent of his charity.

JOS. SURF. My dear sir, you were strangely misinformed. Sir Oliver is a worthy man, a very worthy sort 80 of man; but—avarice, Mr. Stanley, is the vice of age. I will tell you, my good sir, in confidence, what he has done for me has been a mere nothing; though people, I know, have thought otherwise, and, for my part, I never chose to contradict the report.

SIR OLIV. What! has he never transmitted you bullion! rupees! [1] pagodas! [2]

JOS. SURF. O dear sir, nothing of the kind! No, no; a few presents now and then—china—shawls—Congo tea—avadavats[3] and India[n] crackers[4]—little more, believe me.   90

SIR OLIV. [Aside.] Here's gratitude for twelve thousand pounds!—Avadavats and Indian crackers!

JOS. SURF. Then, my dear sir, you have heard, I doubt not, of the extravagance of my brother; there are very few would credit what I have done for that unfortunate young man.

SIR OLIV. Not I, for one!   (Aside.)

JOS. SURF. The sums I have lent him! Indeed I have been exceedingly to blame—it was an amiable weakness: however, I don't pretend to defend it—and 100 now I feel it doubly culpable, since it has deprived me of the pleasure of serving you, Mr. Stanley, as my heart dictates.

SIR OLIV. [Aside.] Dissembler!—Then, sir, you cannot assist me?

JOS. SURF. At present, it grieves me to say, I cannot; but, whenever I have the ability, you may depend upon hearing from me.

SIR OLIV. I am extremely sorry——

JOS. SURF. Not more than I am, believe me; to pity, 110 without the power to relieve, is still more painful than to ask and be denied.

SIR OLIV. Kind sir, your most obedient humble servant.

JOS. SURF. You leave me deeply affected, Mr. Stanley.—William, be ready to open the door.

SIR OLIV. O dear sir, no ceremony.

[1] rupees Indian coins, then worth about two shillings   [2] pagodas Indian coins, then worth about eight shillings   [3] avadavats very small Indian songbirds   [4] India crackers fire crackers

Jos. Surf. Your very obedient.

Sir Oliv. Sir, your most obsequious.

120   Jos. Surf. You may depend upon hearing from me, whenever I can be of service.

Sir Oliv. Sweet sir, you are too good.

Jos. Surf. In the meantime I wish you health and spirits.

Sir Oliv. Your ever grateful and perpetual humble servant.

Jos. Surf. Sir, yours as sincerely.

Sir Oliv. Now I am satisfied!   *Exit.*

Jos. Surf. (*Solus.*) This is one bad effect of a good

130 character; it invites applications from the unfortunate, and there needs no small degree of address to gain the reputation of benevolence without incurring the expense. The silver ore of pure charity is an expensive article in the catalogue of a man's good qualities; whereas the sentimental French plate I use instead of it makes just as good a show, and pays no tax.

Enter Rowley.

Row. Mr. Surface, your servant—I was apprehensive of interrupting you—though my business demands immediate attention—as this note will inform

140 you.

Jos. Surf. Always happy to see Mr. Rowley.— (*Reads.*) How! 'Oliver—Surface!'—My uncle arrived!

Row. He is, indeed—we have just parted—quite well, after a speedy voyage, and impatient to embrace his worthy nephew.

Jos. Surf. I am astonished!—William! stop Mr. Stanley, if he's not gone.

Row. Oh! he's out of reach, I believe.

Jos. Surf. Why didn't you let me know this when

150 you came in together?

Row. I thought you had particular business. But I

must be gone to inform your brother, and appoint him here to meet his uncle. He will be with you in a quarter of an hour.

Jos. Surf. So he says. Well, I am strangely overjoyed at his coming.—(*Aside.*) Never, to be sure, was anything so damned unlucky!

Row. You will be delighted to see how well he looks.

Jos. Surf. Oh! I'm rejoiced to hear it.—(*Aside.*)   160 Just at this time!

Row. I'll tell him how impatiently you expect him.

Jos. Surf. Do, do; pray give my best duty and affection. Indeed, I cannot express the sensations I feel at the thought of seeing him.—[*Exit* Rowley.] Certainly his coming just at this time is the cruellest piece of ill fortune.   *Exit.*

Scene II

At Sir Peter's.

Enter Mrs. Candour *and Maid.*

Maid. Indeed, ma'am, my lady will see nobody at present.

Mrs. Can. Did you tell her it was her friend Mrs. Candour?

Maid. Yes, madam; but she begs you will excuse her.

Mrs. Can. Do go again; I shall be glad to see her, if it be only for a moment, for I am sure she must be in great distress.—   *Exit Maid.*

Dear heart, how provoking; I'm not mistress of half   10 the circumstances! We shall have the whole affair in the newspapers, with the names of the parties at length, before I have dropped the story at a dozen houses.

Enter Sir Benjamin Backbite.

O dear Sir Benjamin! you have heard, I suppose——
    Sir Ben. Of Lady Teazle and Mr. Surface——
    Mrs. Can. And Sir Peter's discovery——
    Sir Ben. Oh, the strangest piece of business, to be sure!
20   Mrs. Can. Well, I never was so surprised in my life. I am so sorry for all parties, indeed I am.
    Sir Ben. Now, I don't pity Sir Peter at all—he was so extravagantly partial to Mr. Surface.
    Mrs. Can. Mr. Surface! Why, 'twas with Charles Lady Teazle was detected.
    Sir Ben. No such thing—Mr. Surface is the gallant.
    Mrs. Can. No, no—Charles is the man. 'Twas Mr. Surface brought Sir Peter on purpose to discover them.
30   Sir Ben. I tell you I have it from one——
    Mrs. Can. And I have it from one——
    Sir Ben. Who had it from one, who had it——
    Mrs. Can. From one immediately—— But here's Lady Sneerwell; perhaps she knows the whole affair.

Enter Lady Sneerwell.

Lady Sneer. So, my dear Mrs. Candour, here's a sad affair of our friend Lady Teazle!
    Mrs. Can. Aye, my dear friend, who could have thought it——
    Lady Sneer. Well, there's no trusting appearances;
40 though, indeed, she was always too lively for me.
    Mrs. Can. To be sure, her manners were a little too free—but she was very young!
    Lady Sneer. And had, indeed, some good qualities.
    Mrs. Can. So she had, indeed. But have you heard the particulars?

LADY SNEER. No; but everybody says that Mr. Surface——

SIR BEN. Aye, there, I told you—Mr. Surface was the man.

MRS. CAN. No, no, indeed—the assignation was with 50 Charles.

LADY SNEER. With Charles! You alarm me, Mrs. Candour.

MRS. CAN. Yes, yes, he was the lover. Mr. Surface—do him justice—was only the informer.

SIR BEN. Well, I'll not dispute with you, Mrs. Candour; but, be it which it may, I hope that Sir Peter's wound will not——

MRS. CAN. Sir Peter's wound! Oh, mercy! I didn't hear a word of their fighting.   60

LADY SNEER. Nor I, a syllable.

SIR BEN. No! what, no mention of the duel?

MRS. CAN. Not a word.

SIR BEN. O Lord—yes, yes—they fought before they left the room.

LADY SNEER. Pray let us hear.

MRS. CAN. Aye, do oblige us with the duel.

SIR BEN. 'Sir,' says Sir Peter—immediately after the discovery—'you are a most ungrateful fellow.'

MRS. CAN. Aye, to Charles——   70

SIR BEN. No, no—to Mr. Surface—'a most ungrateful fellow; and old as I am, sir,' says he, 'I insist on immediate satisfaction.'

MRS. CAN. Aye, that must have been to Charles; for 'tis very unlikely Mr. Surface should go to fight in his house.

SIR BEN. 'Gad's life, ma'am, not at all—'giving me immediate satisfaction.'—On this, madam, Lady Teazle, seeing Sir Peter in such danger, ran out of the room in strong hysterics, and Charles after her, calling out 80 for hartshorn and water! Then, madam, they began to fight with swords——

Enter CRABTREE.

CRAB. With pistols, nephew—I have it from undoubted authority.

MRS. CAN. O Mr. Crabtree, then it is all true!

CRAB. Too true, indeed, ma'am, and Sir Peter's dangerously wounded——

SIR BEN. By a thrust of *in seconde*[5] quite through his
left side——

90   CRAB. By a bullet lodged in the thorax.

MRS. CAN. Mercy on me! Poor Sir Peter!

CRAB. Yes, ma'am—though Charles would have
avoided the matter, if he could.

MRS. CAN. I knew Charles was the person.

SIR BEN. Oh, my uncle, I see, knows nothing of the
matter.

CRAB. But Sir Peter taxed him with the basest ingratitude——

SIR BEN. That I told you, you know.

100   CRAB. Do, nephew, let me speak!—and insisted on
an immediate——

SIR BEN. Just as I said.

CRAB. Odds life, nephew, allow others to know
something too! A pair of pistols lay on the bureau (for
Mr. Surface, it seems, had come the night before late
from Salt-Hill, where he had been to see the Montem[6]
with a friend, who has a son at Eton), so, unluckily,
the pistols were left charged.

SIR BEN. I heard nothing of this.

110   CRAB. Sir Peter forced Charles to take one, and they
fired, it seems, pretty nearly together. Charles's shot
took place, as I told you, and Sir Peter's missed; but,
what is very extraordinary, the ball struck against a
little bronze Pliny that stood over the chimney-piece,
grazed out of the window at a right angle, and

[5] *in seconde* a fencing term   [6] **Montem** a festival celebrated by
the students of Eton at Salt Hill

wounded the postman, who was just coming to the door with a double letter from Northamptonshire.

SIR BEN. My uncle's account is more circumstantial, I must confess; but I believe mine is the true one, for all that.   120

LADY SNEER. [*Aside.*] I am more interested in this affair than they imagine, and must have better information.   *Exit* LADY SNEERWELL.

SIR BEN. (*After a pause looking at each other.*) Ah! Lady Sneerwell's alarm is very easily accounted for.

CRAB. Yes, yes, they certainly *do* say—but that's neither here nor there.

MRS. CAN. But, pray, where is Sir Peter at present?

CRAB. Oh! they brought him home, and he is now in the house, though the servants are ordered to deny 130 it.

MRS. CAN. I believe so, and Lady Teazle, I suppose, attending him.

CRAB. Yes, yes; I saw one of the faculty enter just before me.

SIR BEN. Hey! who comes here?

CRAB. Oh, this is he—the physician, depend on't.

MRS. CAN. Oh, certainly! it must be the physician; and now we shall know.

Enter SIR OLIVER SURFACE.

CRAB. Well, doctor, what hopes?   140

MRS. CAN. Aye, doctor, how's your patient?

SIR BEN. Now, doctor, isn't it a wound with a small-sword?

CRAB. A bullet lodged in the thorax, for a hundred!

SIR OLIV. Doctor! a wound with a small-sword! and a bullet in the thorax?—Oons! are you mad, good people?

SIR BEN. Perhaps, sir, you are not a doctor?

SIR OLIV. Truly, I am to thank you for my degree, if I am.   150

CRAB. Only a friend of Sir Peter's, then, I presume. But, sir, you must have heard of this accident?

SIR OLIV. Not a word!

CRAB. Not of his being dangerously wounded?

SIR OLIV. The devil he is!

SIR BEN. Run through the body——

CRAB. Shot in the breast——

SIR BEN. By one Mr. Surface——

CRAB. Aye, the younger.

160 SIR OLIV. Hey! what the plague! you seem to differ strangely in your accounts—however, you agree that Sir Peter is dangerously wounded.

SIR BEN. Oh, yes, we agree there.

CRAB. Yes, yes, I believe there can be no doubt of that.

SIR OLIV. Then, upon my word, for a person in that situation, he is the most imprudent man alive—for here he comes, walking as if nothing at all were the matter.

Enter SIR PETER TEAZLE.

170 Odds heart, Sir Peter! you are come in good time, I promise you; for we had just *given you over.*

SIR BEN. Egad, uncle, this is the most sudden recovery!

SIR OLIV. Why, man! what do you do out of bed with a small-sword through your body, and a bullet lodged in your thorax?

SIR PET. A small-sword and a bullet?

SIR OLIV. Aye; these gentlemen would have killed you without law or physic, and wanted to dub me a
180 doctor—to make me an accomplice.

SIR PET. Why, what is all this?

SIR BEN. We rejoice, Sir Peter, that the story of the duel is not true, and are sincerely sorry for your other misfortunes.

SIR PET. So, so; all over the town already.   (*Aside.*)

CRAB. Though, Sir Peter, you were certainly vastly
to blame to marry at all, at your years.

SIR PET. Sir, what business is that of yours?

MRS. CAN. Though, indeed, as Sir Peter made so
good a husband, he's very much to be pitied.   190

SIR PET. Plague on your pity, ma'am! I desire none
of it.

SIR BEN. However, Sir Peter, you must not mind the
laughing and jests you will meet with on this occasion.

SIR PET. Sir, I desire to be master in my own house.

CRAB. 'Tis no uncommon case, that's one comfort.

SIR PET. I insist on being left to myself: without
ceremony, I insist on your leaving my house directly!

MRS. CAN. Well, well, we are going; and depend
on't, we'll make the best report of you we can.   200

SIR PET. Leave my house!

CRAB. And tell how hardly you have been treated.

SIR PET. Leave my house!

SIR BEN. And how patiently you bear it.

SIR PET. Fiends! vipers! furies! Oh! that their own
venom would choke them!

Exeunt MRS. CANDOUR, SIR BENJAMIN BACKBITE,
CRABTREE, &C.

SIR OLIV. They are very provoking indeed, Sir Peter.

Enter ROWLEY.

ROW. I heard high words—what has ruffled you,
Sir Peter?

SIR PET. Pshaw! what signifies asking? Do I ever   210
pass a day without my vexations?

SIR OLIV. Well, I'm not inquisitive—I come only to
tell you that I have seen both my nephews in the
manner we proposed.

SIR PET. A precious couple they are!

ROW. Yes, and Sir Oliver is convinced that your
judgment was right, Sir Peter.

Sir Oliv. Yes, I find *Joseph* is indeed the man, after all.

220   Row. Yes, as Sir Peter says, he's a man of sentiment.

Sir Oliv. And acts up to the sentiments he professes.

Row. It certainly is edification to hear him talk.

Sir Oliv. Oh, he's a model for the young men of the age! But how's this, Sir Peter? you don't join in your friend Joseph's praise, as I expected.

Sir Pet. Sir Oliver, we live in a damned wicked world, and the fewer we praise the better.

Row. What! do *you* say so, Sir Peter, who were never mistaken in your life?

230   Sir Pet. Pshaw! plague on you both! I see by your sneering you have heard the whole affair. I shall go mad among you!

Row. Then, to fret you no longer, Sir Peter, we are indeed acquainted with it all. I met Lady Teazle coming from Mr. Surface's, so humbled that she deigned to request me to be her advocate with you.

Sir Pet. And does Sir Oliver know all too?

Sir Oliv. Every circumstance.

Sir Pet. What, of the closet—and the screen, hey?

240   Sir Oliv. Yes, yes, and the little French milliner. Oh, I have been vastly diverted with the story! ha! ha!

Sir Pet. 'Twas very pleasant.

Sir Oliv. I never laughed more in my life, I assure you: ha! ha!

Sir Pet. O, vastly diverting! ha! ha!

Row. To be sure, Joseph with his sentiments! ha! ha!

Sir Pet. Yes, yes, his sentiments! ha! ha! A hypocritical villain!

Sir Oliv. Aye, and that rogue Charles to pull Sir

250   Peter out of the closet: ha! ha!

Sir Pet. Ha! ha! 'twas devilish entertaining, to be sure!

Sir Oliv. Ha! ha! Egad, Sir Peter, I should like to have seen your face when the screen was thrown down: ha! ha!

SIR PET. Yes, yes, my face when the screen was thrown down: ha! ha! Oh, I must never show my head again!

SIR OLIV. But come, come, it isn't fair to laugh at you neither, my old friend— though, upon my soul, I 260 can't help it.

SIR PET. Oh, pray don't restrain your mirth on my account—it does not hurt me at all! I laugh at the whole affair myself. Yes, yes, I think being a standing jest for all one's acquaintances a very happy situation. O yes, and then of a morning to read the paragraphs about Mr. S——, Lady T——, and Sir P——, will be so entertaining!

Row. Without affectation, Sir Peter, you may despise the ridicule of fools. But I see Lady Teazle going 270 towards the next room; I am sure you must desire a reconciliation as earnestly as she does.

SIR OLIV. Perhaps my being here prevents her coming to you. Well, I'll leave honest Rowley to mediate between you; but he must bring you all presently to Mr. Surface's, where I am now returning, if not to reclaim a libertine, at least to expose hypocrisy.

SIR PET. Ah! I'll be present at your discovering yourself there with all my heart—though 'tis a vile unlucky place for discoveries!   280

Row. We'll follow.   [*Exit* SIR OLIVER SURFACE.]

SIR PET. She is not coming here, you see, Rowley.

Row. No, but she has left the door of that room open, you perceive. See, she is in tears!

SIR PET. Certainly a little mortification appears very becoming in a wife! Don't you think it will do her good to let her pine a little?

Row. Oh, this is ungenerous in you!

SIR PET. Well, I know not what to think. You remember, Rowley, the letter I found of hers, evidently 290 intended for Charles!

Row. A mere forgery, Sir Peter! laid in your way

on purpose. This is one of the points which I intend *Snake* shall give you conviction on.

Sɪʀ Pᴇᴛ. I wish I were once satisfied of that. She looks this way. What a remarkably elegant turn of the head she has! Rowley, I'll go to her.

Row. Certainly.

Sɪʀ Pᴇᴛ. Though, when it is known that we are
300 reconciled, people will laugh at me ten times more!

Row. Let them laugh, and retort their malice only by showing them you are happy in spite of it.

Sɪʀ Pᴇᴛ. I'faith, so I will! and, if I'm not mistaken, we may yet be the happiest couple in the country.

Row. Nay, Sir Peter—he who once lays aside suspicion——

Sɪʀ Pᴇᴛ. Hold, my dear Rowley! if you have any regard for me, never let me hear you utter anything like a sentiment—I have had enough of them to serve me
310 the rest of my life.   *Exeunt.*

Sᴄᴇɴᴇ III

The library [in Jᴏsᴇᴘʜ Sᴜʀғᴀᴄᴇ's *house].*

Jᴏsᴇᴘʜ Sᴜʀғᴀᴄᴇ *and* Lᴀᴅʏ Sɴᴇᴇʀᴡᴇʟʟ.

Lᴀᴅʏ Sɴᴇᴇʀ. Impossible! Will not Sir Peter immediately be reconciled to Charles, and of consequence no longer oppose his union with Maria? The thought is distraction to me!

Jᴏs. Sᴜʀғ. Can passion furnish a remedy?

Lᴀᴅʏ Sɴᴇᴇʀ. No, nor cunning either. Oh, I was a fool, an idiot, to league with such a blunderer!

Jᴏs. Sᴜʀғ. Sure, Lady Sneerwell, *I* am the greatest sufferer; yet you see I bear the accident with calmness.
10   Lᴀᴅʏ Sɴᴇᴇʀ. Because the disappointment doesn't reach your *heart;* your *interest* only attached you to Maria. Had you felt for *her* what *I* have for that ungrateful libertine, neither your temper nor hypocrisy

could prevent your showing the sharpness of your vexation.

Jos. Surf. But why should your reproaches fall on *me* for this disappointment?

Lady Sneer. Are you not the cause of it? What had you to do to bate in your pursuit of Maria to pervert Lady Teazle by the way? Had you not a sufficient field 20 for your roguery in blinding Sir Peter, and supplanting your brother? I hate such an avarice of crimes; 'tis an unfair monopoly, and never prospers.

Jos. Surf. Well, I admit I have been to blame. I confess I deviated from the direct road of wrong, but I don't think we're so totally defeated neither.

Lady Sneer. No!

Jos. Surf. You tell me you have made a trial of Snake since we met, and that you still believe him faithful to us— 30

Lady Sneer. I do believe so.

Jos. Surf. And that he has undertaken, should it be necessary, to swear and prove that Charles is at this time contracted by vows and honor to your ladyship —which some of his former letters to you will serve to support?

Lady Sneer. This, indeed, might have assisted.

Jos. Surf. Come, come; it is not too late yet.— [*Knocking at the door.*] But hark! this is probably my uncle, Sir Oliver: retire to that room; we'll consult 40 farther when he's gone.

Lady Sneer. Well! but if *he* should find you out too—

Jos. Surf. Oh, I have no fear of that. Sir Peter will hold his tongue for his own credit['s] sake—and you may depend on't I shall soon discover Sir Oliver's weak side!

Lady Sneer. I have no diffidence of your abilities— only be constant to one roguery at a time.   *Exit.*

Jos. Surf. I will, I will! So! 'tis confounded hard, 50 after such bad fortune, to be baited by one's confed-

erate in evil. Well, at all events, my character is so
much better than Charles's, that I certainly—hey!—
what!—this is not *Sir Oliver*, but old *Stanley* again!
Plague on't! that he should return to tease me just
now! We shall have Sir Oliver come and find him here
—and——

Enter SIR OLIVER SURFACE.

Gad's life, Mr. Stanley, why have you come back to
plague me just at this time? You must not stay now,
60 upon my word.

SIR OLIV. Sir, I hear your uncle Oliver is expected
here, and though he has been so penurious to *you*,
I'll try what he'll do for *me*.

JOS. SURF. Sir, 'tis impossible for you to stay now,
so I must beg—— Come any other time, and I promise
you, you shall be assisted.

SIR OLIV. No: Sir Oliver and I must be acquainted.

JOS. SURF. Zounds, sir! then I insist on your quitting
the room directly.

70   SIR OLIV. Nay, sir!

JOS. SURF. Sir, I insist on't!—Here, William! show
this gentleman out. Since you compel me, sir—not one
moment—this is such insolence!

(*Going to push him out.*)

Enter CHARLES SURFACE.

CHAS. SURF. Heyday! what's the matter now? What
the devil, have you got hold of my little broker here?
Zounds, brother, don't hurt little Premium. What's the
matter, my little fellow?

JOS. SURF. So! he has been with you, too, has he?

CHAS. SURF. To be sure he has! Why, 'tis as honest
80 a little—— But sure, Joseph, you have not been borrowing money too, have you?

JOS. SURF. Borrowing! no! But, brother, you know
here we expect Sir Oliver every——

CHAS. SURF. O gad, that's true! Noll mustn't find the little broker here, to be sure.

JOS. SURF. Yet, Mr. *Stanley* insists——

CHAS. SURF. Stanley! why his name is *Premium*.

JOS. SURF. No, no, *Stanley*.

CHAS. SURF. No, no, *Premium*.

JOS. SURF. Well, no matter which—but—— 90

CHAS. SURF. Aye, aye, Stanley or Premium, 'tis the same thing, as you say; for I suppose he goes by half [a] hundred names, besides A.B.'s at the coffee-houses.

JOS. SURF. Death! here's Sir Oliver at the door. (*Knocking again.*) Now I beg, Mr. Stanley——

CHAS. SURF. Aye, and I beg, Mr. Premium——

SIR OLIV. Gentlemen——

JOS. SURF. Sir, by heaven you shall go!

CHAS. SURF. Aye, out with him, certainly.

SIR OLIV. This violence—— 100

JOS. SURF. 'Tis your own fault.

CHAS. SURF. Out with him, to be sure.

(*Both forcing* SIR OLIVER *out.*)

Enter SIR PETER *and* LADY TEAZLE, MARIA, *and* ROWLEY.

SIR PET. My old friend, Sir Oliver—hey! What in the name of wonder!—Here are dutiful nephews!—assault their uncle at the first visit!

LADY TEAZ. Indeed, Sir Oliver, 'twas well we came in to rescue you.

ROW. Truly it was; for I perceive, Sir Oliver, the character of old Stanley was no protection to you.

SIR OLIV. Nor of Premium either: the necessities of 110 the *former* could not extort a shilling from *that* benevolent gentleman; and now, egad, I stood a chance of faring worse than my ancestors, and being knocked down without being bid for.

(*After a pause,* JOSEPH *and* CHARLES *turning to each other.*)

Jos. Surf. Charles!

Chas. Surf. Joseph!

Jos. Surf. 'Tis now complete!

Chas. Surf. Very!

Sir Oliv. Sir Peter, my friend, and Rowley too—
120 look on that elder nephew of mine. You know what
he has already received from my bounty; and you
know also how gladly I would have regarded half my
fortune as held in trust for him—judge, then, my disappointment in discovering him to be destitute of
truth—charity—and gratitude!

Sir Pet. Sir Oliver, I should be more surprised at
this declaration, if I had not myself found him selfish,
treacherous, and hypocritical!

Lady Teaz. And if the gentleman pleads not guilty
130 to these, pray let him call *me* to his character.

Sir Pet. Then, I believe, we need add no more.—
if he knows himself, he will consider it as the most
perfect punishment that he is known to the world.

Chas. Surf. (*Aside.*) If they talk this way to *Hon-
esty*, what will they say to *me*, by and by?

(Sir Peter, Lady Teazle, *and* Maria *retire.*)

Sir Oliv. As for that prodigal, his brother, there——

Chas. Surf. (*Aside.*) Aye, now comes my turn: the
damned family pictures will ruin me!

Jos. Surf. Sir Oliver!—uncle!—will you honor me
140 with a hearing?

Chas. Surf. (*Aside.*) Now if Joseph would make
one of his long speeches, I might recollect myself a
little.

Sir Oliv. [*to* Joseph Surface]. I suppose you would
undertake to justify yourself entirely?

Jos. Surf. I trust I could.

Sir Oliv. Pshaw!—Well, sir! and *you* (*to* Charles)
could justify yourself too, I suppose?

Chas. Surf. Not that I know of, Sir Oliver.

150   Sir Oliv. What!—Little Premium has been let too
much into the secret, I presume?

CHAS. SURF. True, sir; but they were family secrets, and should never be mentioned again, you know.

Row. Come, Sir Oliver, I know you cannot speak of Charles's follies with anger.

SIR OLIV. Odd's heart, no more I can—nor with gravity either. Sir Peter, do you know the rogue bargained with me for all his ancestors—sold me judges and generals by the foot—and maiden aunts as cheap as broken china. 160

CHAS. SURF. To be sure, Sir Oliver, I did make a little free with the family canvas, that's the truth on't. My ancestors may certainly rise in evidence against me, there's no denying it; but believe me sincere when I tell you—and upon my soul I would not say it if I was not that if I do not appear mortified at the exposure of my follies, it is because I feel at this moment the warmest satisfaction in seeing you, my liberal benefactor.

SIR OLIV. Charles, I believe you. Give me your hand 170 again; the ill-looking little fellow over the settee has made your peace.

CHAS. SURF. Then, sir, my gratitude to the original is still increased.

LADY TEAZ. (*Pointing to* MARIA.) Yet, I believe, Sir Oliver, here is one whom Charles is still more anxious to be reconciled to.

SIR OLIV. Oh, I have heard of his attachment there; and, with the young lady's pardon, if I construe right —that blush—— 180

SIR PET. Well, child, speak your sentiments.

MARIA. Sir, I have little to say, but that I shall rejoice to hear that he is happy; for me, whatever claim I had to his affection, I willingly resign it to one who has a better title.

CHAS. SURF. How, Maria!

SIR PET. Heyday! what's the mystery now? While he appeared an incorrigible rake, you would give your

hand to no one else; and now that he is likely to re-
190 form, I warrant you won't have him.

MARIA. His own heart—and Lady Sneerwell know
the cause.

CHAS. SURF. Lady Sneerwell!

JOS. SURF. Brother, it is with great concern I am
obliged to speak on this point, but my regard to justice
compels me, and Lady Sneerwell's injuries can no
longer be concealed.   (*Goes to the door.*)

Enter LADY SNEERWELL.

SIR PET. So! another French milliner!—Egad, he
has one in every room in the house, I suppose!
200 LADY SNEER. Ungrateful Charles! Well may you be
surprised, and feel for the indelicate situation which
your perfidy has forced me into.

CHAS. SURF. Pray, uncle, is this another plot of
yours? For, as I have life, I don't understand it.

JOS. SURF. I believe, sir, there is but the evidence of
one person more necessary to make it extremely clear.

SIR PET. And that person, I imagine, is Mr. Snake.
—Rowley, you were perfectly right to bring him with
us, and pray let him appear.
210 Row. Walk in, Mr. Snake.

Enter SNAKE.

I thought his testimony might be wanted; however, it
happens unluckily, that he comes to confront Lady
Sneerwell, and not to support her.

LADY SNEER. Villain! Treacherous to me at last!
(*Aside.*)—Speak, fellow, have *you* too conspired
against me?

SNAKE. I beg your ladyship ten thousand pardons:
you paid me extremely liberally for the lie in question;
but I have unfortunately been offered double to speak
220 the truth.

SIR PET. Plot and counterplot, egad—I wish your ladyship joy of the success of your negotiation.

LADY SNEER. The torments of shame and disappointment on you all!

LADY TEAZ. Hold, Lady Sneerwell—before you go, let me thank you for the trouble you and that gentleman have taken, in writing letters to me from Charles, and answering them yourself; and let me also request you to make my respects to the Scandalous College, of which you are president, and inform them, that 230 Lady Teazle, licentiate, begs leave to return the diploma they granted her, as she leaves off practice, and kills characters no longer.

LADY SNEER. You too, madam!—provoking—insolent! May your husband live these fifty years!   *Exit.*

SIR PET. Oons! what a fury!

LADY TEAZ. A malicious creature, indeed!

SIR PET. Hey! not for her last wish?

LADY TEAZ. Oh, no!

SIR OLIV. Well, sir, and what have you to say now?   240

JOS. SURF. Sir, I am so confounded, to find that Lady *Sneerwell* could be guilty of suborning Mr. *Snake* in this manner, to impose on us all, that I know not what to say; however, lest her revengeful spirit should prompt her to injure my brother, I had certainly better follow her directly.   *Exit.*

SIR PET. Moral to the last drop!

SIR OLIV. Aye, and marry her, Joseph, if you can. —Oil and vinegar, egad! you'll do very well together.

ROW. I believe we have no more occasion for Mr. 250 Snake at present.

SNAKE. Before I go, I beg pardon once for all, for whatever uneasiness I have been the humble instrument of causing to the parties present.

SIR PET. Well, well, you have made atonement by a good deed at last.

SNAKE. But I must request of the company, that it shall never be known.

Sir Pet. Hey! what the plague! are you ashamed of
260 having done a right thing once in your life?

Snake. Ah, sir,—consider I live by the badness of
my character—I have nothing but my infamy to depend on! and, if it were once known that I had been
betrayed into an honest action, I should lose every
friend I have in the world.

Sir Oliv. Well, well—we'll not traduce you by saying anything in your praise, never fear.   *Exit* Snake.

Sir Pet. There's a precious rogue! yet that fellow is
a writer and a critic!

270   Lady Teaz. See, Sir Oliver, there needs no persua-
sion now to reconcile your nephew and Maria.

(Charles *and* Maria *apart.*)

Sir Oliv. Aye, aye, that's as it should be, and, egad,
we'll have the wedding to-morrow morning.

Chas. Surf. Thank you, my dear uncle.

Sir Pet. What, you rogue! don't you ask the girl's
consent first?

Chas. Surf. Oh, I have done that a long time—
above a minute ago—and she has looked yes.

Maria. For shame, Charles!—I protest, Sir Peter,
280 there has not been a word——

Sir Oliv. Well, then, the fewer the better—may
your love for each other never know abatement.

Sir Pet. And may you live as happily together as
Lady Teazle and I—intend to do!

Chas. Surf. Rowley, my old friend, I am sure you
congratulate me; and I suspect that I owe you much.

Sir Oliv. You do, indeed, Charles.

Row. If my efforts to serve you had not succeeded
you would have been in my debt for the attempt—
290 but deserve to be happy—and you overpay me.

Sir Pet. Aye, honest Rowley always said you would
reform.

Chas. Surf. Why as to reforming, Sir Peter, I'll
make no promises, and that I take to be a proof that
I intend to set about it.—But here shall be my monitor

—my gentle guide.—Ah! can I leave the virtuous path
those eyes illumine?

Though thou, dear maid, shouldst wa[i]ve thy *beauty's*
    sway,
Thou still must rule, because I *will* obey:
An humbled fugitive from Folly view,   300
No sanctuary near but *Love* and—You;

                          (*To the audience.*)

    You can, indeed, each anxious fear remove,
    For even *Scandal* dies, if *you* approve.
                Finis.

EPILOGUE

WRITTEN BY G. COLMAN, ESQ.[1]

SPOKEN BY MRS. ABINGTON[2]

I, who was late so volatile and gay,
Like a trade-wind must now blow all one way,
Bend all my cares, my studies, and my vows,
To one old rusty weathercock—my spouse!
So wills our virtuous bard—the motley Bayes[3]
Of crying epilogues and laughing plays!

  Old bachelors, who marry smart young wives,
Learn from our play to regulate your lives:
Each bring his dear to town, all faults upon her—
London will prove the very source of honor.   10
Plunged fairly in, like a cold bath it serves,
When principles relax, to brace the nerves.

  Such is my case;—and yet I might deplore
That the gay dream of dissipation's o'er;
And say, ye fair, was ever lively wife,
Born with a genius for the highest life,
Like me untimely blasted in her bloom,
Like me condemned to such a dismal doom?
Save money—when I just knew how to waste it!
Leave London—just as I began to taste it!   20
Must I then watch the early crowing cock,
The melancholy ticking of a clock;
In the lone rustic hall for ever pounded,
With dogs, cats, rats, and squalling brats surrounded?
With humble curates can I now retire,
(While good Sir Peter boozes with the squire,)
And at backgammon mortify my soul,

---

[1] **G. Colman, Esq.** the dramatist, George Colman the elder (1732-1794)   [2] **Mrs. Abington** Frances Abington, who had the role of Lady Teazle   [3] **Bayes** alluding to the dramatist burlesqued in the Duke of Buckingham's *The Rehearsal*

That pants for loo,[4] or flutters at a vole?[5]
Seven's the main![6] Dear sound!—that must expire,
30 Lost at hot cockles,[7] round a Christmas fire!
The transient hour of fashion too soon spent,
Farewell the tranquil mind, farewell content![8]
Farewell the plumèd head, the cushioned tête,
That takes the cushion from its proper seat!
That spirit-stirring drum![9]—card drums I mean,
Spadille[10]—odd trick—pam[11]—basto[12]—king and
    queen!
And you, ye knockers, that, with brazen throat,
The welcome visitors' approach denote;
Farewell! all quality of high renown,
40 Pride, pomp, and circumstance of glorious town!
Farewell! your revels I partake no more,
And Lady Teazle's occupation's o'er!
All this I told our bard—he smiled, and said 'twas clear,
I ought to play deep tragedy next year.
Meanwhile he drew wise morals from his play,
And in these solemn periods stalked away:—
'Blest were the fair like you; her faults who stopped,
And closed her follies when the curtain dropped!
No more in vice or error to engage,
50 Or play the fool at large on life's great stage.'

[4] loo a card game   [5] vole the winning of all the tricks   [6] Seven's
the main a term in the game of hazard   [7] hot cockles a country
game   [8] Farewell . . . occupation's o'er! these lines parody a
soliloquy of Othello, III.iii.347-357   [9] drum an evening party
at a private house   [10] Spadille ace of spades   [11] pam jack of
clubs   [12] basto ace of clubs

SELECTED BIBLIOGRAPHY

BIOGRAPHY

Moore, Thomas, *Memoirs of the Life of the Right Honourable Richard Brinsley Sheridan*, 2 vols. (London, 1825).

Rhodes, R. Crompton, *Harlequin Sheridan: The Man and the Legends* (Oxford, 1933).

Sichel, Walter, *Sheridan*, 2 vols. (London, 1909).

TEXTS AND DISCUSSION OF TEXTS

Nettleton, George H., and Arthur E. Case, *British Dramatists from Dryden to Sheridan* (Boston, 1939). Prints *The School for Scandal* from the manuscript which Sheridan presented to Mrs. Crewe. Nettleton (pp. 951-955) summarizes the bibliographical history of the play.

Rae, W. F., ed., *Sheridan's Plays Now Printed as He Wrote Them* (London, 1902). Prints *The School for Scandal* from a manuscript showing the play in an earlier form than that of its first production.

Rhodes, R. Crompton, *The Plays and Poems of Richard Brinsley Sheridan*, 3 vols. (Oxford, 1928).

Van Lennep, William, "The Chetwynd Manuscript of *The School for Scandal*," *Theatre Notebook*, VI (1951), 10-12. Describes the copy made about May 1, 1777, for the licenser of plays.

BACKGROUND AND CRITICISM

Bernbaum, Ernest, *The Drama of Sensibility* (Boston, 1915).

Crane, Ronald S., "Suggestions Towards a Genealogy of the 'Man of Feeling,'" *ELH, A Journal of English Literary History*, I (1934), 205-230.

Kronenberger, Louis, *The Thread of Laughter: Chapters on English Stage Comedy from Jonson to Maugham* (New York, 1952).

Krutch, Joseph Wood, *Comedy and Conscience after the Restoration* (New York, 1924).

Lynch, James J., *Box, Pit, and Gallery: Stage and Society in Johnson's London* (Berkeley and Los Angeles, 1953).

Nettleton, George H., *English Drama of the Restoration and Eighteenth Century (1642-1780)* (New York, 1914).

Nicoll, Allardyce, *A History of Late Eighteenth Century Drama* (Cambridge, 1952).

Tave, Stuart M., *The Amiable Humorist: A Study in the Comic Theory and Criticism of the Eighteenth and Early Nineteenth Centuries* (Chicago, 1960).